LEGAL

First

21

YEARS

LEGAL

THE First 21 YEARS

JONATHAN
WALTON

TATE PUBLISHING & Enterprises

Published by Tate Publishing & Enterprises, LLC
127 E. Trade Center Terrace | Mustang, Oklahoma 73064 USA
1.888.361.9473 | www.tatepublishing.com

Tate Publishing is committed to excellence in the publishing industry. The company reflects the philosophy established by the founders, based on Psalm 68:11,
"The Lord gave the word and great was the company of those who published it."

Published in the United States of America

ISBN: 978-1-60604-573-2
1. Poetry: General
2. Political Science: Political Ideologies
08.07.14

To you

Hanna,

God Bless you
Amen

9/30/07

Table of Contents

*Indicates a poem commissioned by Poetic People Power.

Foreword

It has been said that the best introduction to a writer's work is the work itself. One opens the pages of a book and begins to read and in that moment one is introduced to the world as the writer sees it.

The world that Jonathan Walton sees and limns so beautifully on these pages is one of contradiction and change, confidence and confusion. It is a world awash in the magical shifting of intellect and emotion that define adolescence, a world in which young people try on selves like clothing, trying to find something that fits through the shoulders and the butt, something that is long enough to cover youthful ankles, short enough to show off youthful knees, a self that is stylish but real. This world of the young is not an easy one to negotiate and few people know it better than Jonathan Walton. Yet even amidst the changing of time and fashion, the fluctuating of moral focus, Mr. Walton found his center and his strength in the voice his God provided.

It is that voice—raw and real and rhythmic, eloquent and poetic, wise and inspiring—that speaks from the

My Release

Poetry is my release
my shield from all grief
my refuge to which I retreat
when this world is too much for me
These phrases on these pages
are the language my mind speaks
metaphors and similes
poetic elements I just—
b r e a t h e
Phrases are written within me
my spirit on this page is free
I see my dreams
I build my fantasies
I am the author
of my own reality
Couplets and quatrains
bleed free within my veins
Sssssshhhhh …
just listen to what my soul is saying
I conspire to inspire

tie words that make you cry
then bind lines in rhyme
that are sure to make you smile
my pens indent white pages
back and forth in smooth strokes
white paper comparable
to ivory keys on a piano
because poetry is my release
I use words and words use me
I am words and words are me
and to express them
is my only dream

Because I will write—I will write,
When I'm tired, hungry, crying or inspired
happy, sad, relaxed, and riled
I will write when I'm used, abused, and confused,
whether or not I'm in the presence of my muse
I will write when I'm warm, cold, lonely, and scolded,
whether or not I have someone to hold me
I will grab an ink-filled pitcher
That you all call a fountain pen
and pour out the lyrical liquid from my soul
because if I don't, I will explode

My hand is filled with heartfelt passion fruit
drank by thirsty paper like ver-
bal vitamin filled orange juice

Because between blue lines
is the boundary of my mind
and with my rhymes I try to move mankind
A constant river of rhymes is flowing inside me
an always high-tided geyser that rises higher and higher
From my soul to my bones, then to that pen that I hold
my stream of consciousness bubbles and overflows
A psychological bombardment
transferred to lead hardened
as my methodical motions make indentions
on indigo marked parchment

Random thoughts vex my intellect
swirl around my head like swarms of insects
I hear dogs barking, angels harking
I see fireworks sparkling, real stars falling
Harps, larks, frosted strawberry pop tarts
Feel swinging hips as hip hop tops pop
and rock on billboard charts
Lyrics transcend uncolored minds and hearts

Rock guitarists rap, rap stars play guitars
Rappers bragging of acquired scars,
Boasting of time spent behind bars
Some people think it's so cool to have entry wounds
Bullet riddled, twice addicted, now afflicted icons
are our idol superstars
Drugs and drinks are enclosed by minks
as fine clothes cloak the conflicts of rich folk
I then focus my attention on ordinary citizens
Gathered in a residence and forced to make decisions
Made to engage in senseless competition
Followed by cameras in pivotal positions
This weekly ritual is called reality television

Private parts of people's lives
are staged, paraded, and amplified
Recorded, reported, televised
Supposed survivors strive to be idolized
I pass big brothers, jump fear factors
wannabe singers, actors, and millionaire benefactors
just to see a new series by MTV
When will we be first class versions of ourselves
and stop being second rate shells of someone else

Dismiss negativity, embrace positivity
and not be, but be like, those pillars of history
Work hard like those figures in documentaries
Seek our destinies and be the people
that we were meant to be
These words, this poetry is my release
my shield from all grief
my refuge to which I retreat
when this world is too much for me
These phrases on these pages
are the language my mind speaks
Metaphors and similes
poetic elements, I just–
b r e a t h e

Now I Am Found

But you are a chosen generation, a royal priesthood, a holy nation, His own special people, that you may proclaim the praises of Him who called you out of darkness into His marvelous light.

1 Peter 2:9 (NIV)

Life is Full

Life is full of decisions
different situations
and compromising positions
Life is an unending game
that we all must play
Mistakes in order to learn
must be made
but the prize is the promise
of each and every day
Life is a constant learning experience
periods of confession
but also of innocence
Times for forgiveness
but also for repentance
each lesson carrying with it
a certain level of significance
Life is a myriad of ups and downs
mountains and valleys forever to be found
but if and when obstacles are met
We must press on and never forget

Each stumbling block is laid
only to make you stronger
granting you the resilience
needed to take you that much farther
Trials and tribulations
are only a part of life
experiencing darkness
only to further enjoy the light
Now be strong in the Lord
and in the power of His might
and with faith in Him
you **will** stand in any fight
No matter your obstacles
however great or small
With faith in God
you will conquer all
Though the world
may fall around you
and only chaos surround you
Havoc hangs in every way
and storms swirl about you—
Be strong and stand
on the promises of God
and He will accompany you down
all of the roads you trod

A Reason

There is a reason for everything
for every occurrence under the sun
without Him no action is halted
and by Him all endeavors are begun
Every triumph and tragedy on the earth
Each happening around the globe
a specific motive it possesses
a particular purpose it holds
No bird sings without His beckoning
No creation is conjured without his reckoning
Each act of nature is etched in His eternal plan
For God clasps the world
in the palm of His mighty hand

One Thing Is Certain

In an instant, reality can be shattered
chaotic occurrences leaving thoughts scattered
acquired wages, by thieves can be taken
fires may erupt and extinguish locations
In the blink of an eye,
man-made elements can be stricken from sight
cyclones, tornados, tsunamis, typhoons
accidents, natural disasters, will and do ensue
With no moment's notice,
worldly possessions can be removed

For nothing earthly is certain to be permanent
only God's love in this universe
has a forever open curtain
residing on an eternal stage,
an immaculate actor in an infinite play
The script never changing, always another page
for all things of this world will soon pass away
but God and His Word will always be the same

Life fades with age, innocence grays with temptation
popular songs are laid in, then taken from rotation
but God's verses survive without a radio station
they thrive in minds and always give inspiration
Childhood is only a phase, adolescence has its days
a young lady blossoms into a woman
and a young boy matures into a man with age
But ask them in later days,
all trends return from whence they came
but they can quote the words to "Amazing Grace"
God's love, His Son, His Word, the Trinity
have no limits, are omniscient,
and live two times eternity.

Now I Am Found

I have reached a crossroad
and I don't know where to turn
I have to go forward, never back
because all of my bridges were burned
I left my friends behind
and now I am left with nothing
abandoned by my family
and now I am searching for something

Everything I do seems to fail
with every goal set, I come up short
I look around in every direction
and there is no support
I have been running this race
but the strain I can no longer take
there is no reason to continue
I am haunted by past mistakes
In the back of my mind I am thinking
will my life end this way?
my heart and soul unowned

my path as dark as a cave
Each day, I awake to a struggle
my skies gray with despair
the sun, hidden behind clouds of doubt
the sound of emptiness in the air

There is a mirror in the bathroom
but I cannot stand to look in the glass
I see my face in standing water
and I have to make a splash
But as I look out of a high-story window
I hear the sound of a ringing church bell
it calls me to its doors
like a thirst-filled worker to a well
As I enter the doors
the organ and guitar were acoustic
but the message of the preacher
was sweeter than the music
He spoke to those who sought spiritual strength
those searching for fulfillment
His message was for sinners
to fall upon their knees and repent
Not because I was wrong

or because someone had been keep-
ing a tally from above
but because Jesus had died for me
purely out of Love
He had humbled Himself
allowed Himself to be hurt
so that through Him I would know true peace
when it was time to leave this Earth
Though I sat on the back row
the words echoed in my soul

There was a light at the end of this tunnel
at the altar that light was shown
But when he called for the altar prayer
I was glued completely to my chair
something inside was holding me back
something would not let my soul be spared
I was not saved that Sunday
but it planted a seed in my heart

I ventured back to that place
where my fulfillment had its start
I accepted a forgiving God
on a cool December afternoon

I was no longer held back by doubt
for I was seated on the very first pew
That day I confessed my sins
and on that day I was forgiven
I felt the burdens fly away from me
Like frightened birds out of a tree
The next week was my baptism
at a quiet place, on the Chesapeake Bay
and when I went underwater
my sins were washed away
I arose a brand new creature
a saved and faithful soul
For I had not a doubt in my mind
that God had made me whole

Only A Man

How can a form of dirt, dust, and water
possibly comprehend the creation
or the blowing of the wind
Man can only hypothesize, he will never know
Man can only plant the seed
never could he make it grow
How can a mound of a trillion cells
reproduce the structure of water
man cannot, he can only dig the well
Man can unite with woman to make a child
but no man can give that young one breath,
or start the small heart within its little chest
Man can only live on this Earth
which was created for him
Man can only take that which was given
Man can consume the pea
but he could not create the pod
Man is only man, but God is God

By Grace

I find myself standing there—gazing into space. No focus, just blank—no expression on my face. No sound proceeded out of my mouth because words could not describe my experience. So I took a pen and I wrote it down. I lost control only sixteen years old, instead of the break, the gas I did hold. I was propelled through the air onto new ground, moving without direction until by grace I was found. God steadied my path, breathed air into my gasp. He gave me another chance when it looked like my last. I flew through the air on a Harley Davidson, over an embankment and into parking spaces. To the left I leaned and then to the right—then I careened to a stop as if at a red light.

I should be lying there, lifeless on the pavement. The subject of police statements with my face plastered on front pages of newspapers, but instead I was spared. "It's not your time," God said, and for me to walk without care would be like exclaiming He wasn't there; because I put fear in the ones most dear to me but it also put a new fear in me. Not the fear of the motorcycle because that is not the lesson. The lesson is that of all things we must be respectful. On this globe we have few moments and in moments all of our moments can be stolen, so I must cherish these moments as if they are something golden; but more than gold. Because you cannot compare life to stone. That would be like saying clothes are worth more than bones, hair is worth less than the comb, the kite is more significant than the wind that blows it. Glasses are more important than sight, the cause is less important than the fight, the ability to speak is more important than a dumb person being able to sign that they are alive. I must view life from a different perspective, look into my reflection and begin inspection, respect the blessings that I have been given—be thankful for my bed but be more thankful to have risen. This lesson I have learned and now I must teach. It's my duty to tell everyone in this world that I see, don't be concerned about the price of your shoes because if you look down you have two feet. Don't worry if you eat hot dogs or the finest beef because on our plates before us we all have something to eat. We all have something worth more than all of Wall Street and it could not be bought with all of this world's currency—a possession greater than any wealth on this planet—a force stronger than any boulder of pure granite.

Each and every one of us has life. An aspect of being that is not fully understood, but living is something that we all must do. We are all people pebbles tossed into a pool, every ripple I create, in turn will ripple you. So in unison we are rippling a type of ripple rhythm but we need to ripple in a way that benefits our living. Actions that hinder our growth are unneeded so we learn from our accidents, they help us in succeeding. Mistakes are necessary but all of our repeats are not. If a ripple that we make is wrong, we should make that ripple stop.

So what will we do with our lives after God has opened our eyes, will we turn our backs and hide from the light or just bathe in its radiance with an enlightened mind.

I Believe Because He Did

My granddaddy taught me that his word was bond
nouns and verbs converted to cash and coins
and put food on the table many a time—
promises got food

A ring around the moon was called a sundog
it meant definite snow the following day
now snowbirds show for no reason, no signal.
silent cries for help

Mother nature says not, *my kids stress me out*
but I find myself asking what if she were
and if she is nearing the end of her nerves
can she take much more

Postmodern man believes that God did exist
but only because the world wanted him to
also, that there is no absolute truth
is that absolute?

We are headed towards a veiled destruction
holding our own hands to cover our own eyes
screaming to the masses that we see all clearly
a drunk world with keys

Granddaddy knew God before the Scriptures
and had a relationship with the land
steward over his own Garden of Eden
plain and important

My granddaddy is dead now and so are his
ideals. Hidden under his coffin pillow.
Too bad that exhumation is illegal.
could save the world.

My granddaddy taught me that his word was bond
A ring around the moon he called a sundog
it meant definite snow the following day
could save the world.

Talitha-Comi

Faith today is vanity
false believers participants
in man-made Christianity
Christians today are walking contradictions
steadfast hypocrites
attempting to reside on both sides of the fence
knowing full-well you can't mix oil and water
the same goes for mingling flesh and spirit

We want to pitch and hit, catch and swing
but we must know that we can't play for both teams

We are God's creations
fashioned and formed in His own image
but now the world has changed
and we in turn wish to change Him

If those in the world
cannot find holiness in the church
to whom will they turn to quench their spiritual thirst

The image of religion is that preach-
ers wish to fill their pockets
snatching dollars to deposit
praising God for a profit
Talented speakers pin flyers and pitch tents
God Himself they represent
then ask for your rent money
because they need that ten percent

Jesus teaches
a heart cannot serve two masters
First chapter of James
a double-minded man is unstable in all his ways
Joshua looked out to his people
and said choose whom you will serve, this day

I choose Jesus Christ
because He is The Way, The Truth and The Life
the sole reason I can smile amid all of my strife
My suffering brings tears
but I have blessed peace and no fear
because when I close my eyes the last time
my father in Heaven is waiting when I leave here
Jesus said Talitha-Comi

meaning damsel I say arise
I use the same phrase
true believers arise
before we raise our eyes and True Christianity has died
Dismiss false teaching preachers
for they preach to your itching ears
in tongues they speak,
saying exactly what you want to hear
Talitha-Comi—faith will always conquer fear
With God lighting your path
the way is always clear
Kill the confusion
heaven and hell are not illusions
the world is in disarray
because God is not included
Baptists, Catholics, Seventh-day Adventists
Hindus, Muslims, Taoists, Jehovah's Witness
Jews, Gentiles, Agnostics, Buddhists,
Methodists, Heretics, Atheists.... excuse this
Forget these denominations
sand-line Sabbath separations
Jesus is Salvation
the only way for us to escape damnation
Talitha-Comi, we must let our lights shine

we are perfect by no means
but in darkness, we must be the Light.

Memorial Day

Memorial Day is an opportunity
to remember this country's unity
to reflect upon our united continuity
Old Glory, the Bald Eagle, and our Constitution
Memorial Day opens our eyes
to the millions of soldiers who have
made the ultimate sacrifice
Families were separated, friends were left behind
Parents left sons and daughters, husbands left wives
They dropped all they had, leaving mom and dad
said goodbye to cousins and kids
not knowing whether or not if they
were to see them again
Some left occupations, others forsook higher education
endured vigorous physical train-
ing and vowed to defend this nation
Traded small towns and cities for bar-
racks and battle stations
that we may have freedom of press, reli-
gion, and elect our own statesmen

They fought for our children, that
they may still hope and dream
and aspire to be, what they choose to be
They fought for those not yet conceived
so that when they live, they could experience democracy
They defended the defenseless, fought for the feeble
they fought regardless of race, for the
right of American people.
They battled for the blind, bled for
friends and strangers alike
fought so that our kids could ride their bikes
fought so that we would be free to pray at night
Soldiers disregard personal opinions
and no matter inner feelings, attempt
to complete their missions
They fought for the causes whether or
not they deemed it necessary
the burden of this country, they all have carried
So with a straight back and a heartfelt salute
I say in a fervent breath, I will pray for you.

Tonight I look to you dear God
to watch over our men and women abroad
Those in the service with their lives on the line

Give them strength in trials
and the courage to fight
Give them sound minds
to perform upright actions
and dear God when it's over
Please bring them back to us
Give peace to the mothers
with strong sons overseas
and console the father
whose daughter he will never see
Give them blessed insight
to see your holy will
and that with your grace
their hearts may be filled
Lord be on the battlefield
and stay with those men and women
for we see not their situations
or know the trouble they have been in
But I know that you see all
and with your limitless sight
You can be right beside them
through light of day and dark of night
Forever bless them
forever keep them

and if it be your will
safe—may we see them.

Amen

Restless Souls

A restless soul cannot sleep
nor can a troubled mind dream
no more than a broken heart beat
and a flooded lung breathe

Heads crowded with emotion
as one lays down to rest
toss and turn in weariness
and find no position best

For the mind is so disturbed
that peace is made improbable
and to wake before the break of dawn
is made all the more possible

So think not on those things
that move thee to anger
Shun these evil thoughts and notions
To your mind—make them strangers

For a soul made restless
shall not find the peace to sleep
and a troubled mind will never reach
the dwelling place of dreams

Little Wooden Church

This is the way it used to be
before pastors were broadcast on TV
and people tried to feel the spirit
through hotlines and television screens

Congregations gathered despite rain, sleet, or snow
because hearing the word of God was worth it
that little talk with Jesus would reach
deep into their struggles
and pour peace into those places
shaken by the uncertainty
of sharecropping in the segregated South.

Church was the only place that you could go
to get meat for your belly, bread for your soul
and living water for your throat

Horses hitched to buggies
and cartwheels cart-wheeled down dirt roads

to meet big women singing songs of Zion
trying to sing the cold away
from hearts that were heavy
and hands that had worked fields all week

Kids weren't sent to separate rooms
they learned how to sit in pews
and discipline was handed out
like peppermint candy from any old hand
that saw fit to put an end to acting up

There was integrity in the room
and words carried weight
because honesty was the only option
bearing false witness meant you
were a liar for a long time—
the Ten Commandments hung on house walls
and were etched on hearts unedited

Under a white-washed steeple
these were God's people
doing their best to close their eyes and see Him
through blinding poverty
and what the first world now calls subsistence farming

Seeing a history of His provision
when they closed their eyes in prayer
Standing the tallest when they hit their knees
and touching generations when
they placed palms together
heads bowed laying burdens down
and offering up all to Him on the altar
because He was the only one that
could make the rains come.

They saw God
in patches of cotton and cabbage
in the blooming of blossoms to apples
in the green grass, brown cows
and each morning's white milk

They saw the Creator's fingerprints
on each piece of their lives
and heard His voice on the breeze
saying, "Don't worry, a harvest is coming—
I am Jehovah-Jireh, Shalom, Nissi, and Raffa
your Provider, your Peace, your Banner, your Healer,
I am."

True Promises

Across the horizon
droplets fall through the air
and with each refraction of light
a banner of promise hangs there
For lofted in heavens
birthed by the sunshine
is a beautiful colored bow
that stretches across the sky
God pledged to Noah
never again would He make a rain
that would pound and flood the Earth
for forty nights and forty days
That promise has not been broken
since the instance it was shown
God has not flooded the globe
since He formed that first rainbow
So let our promises also
remain as true as the tides
and our promises as constant
as that first blessed sign

For the Lost

We need to pray, pray—say a little prayer for peace,
We need to fall down on our knees and pray…
Father in heaven,
the trajectory of this world's moral
standards troubles me
as religion and travesty reverse roles so suddenly
What's right seems wrong and
what's wrong seems right
as if it's fine to see the sun high at
the stroke of midnight
or the moon shine in the noonday sky
Where is the appreciation for the blessing we call life
and the love for each other that
gave the Earth such light

Lord bless those who spend every
night with a different someone
and those who drink until they throw up
Comfort those stricken with disease
and those who must live with HIV

Be with the poor mother at the abortion clinic
and the one who must place her
pen on adoption papers
Be with those persons who tonight will overdose
be by the bedsides of those who lay comatose
Dwell in the hearts of those convicted felons
Let them know that there is something better
Be with that child who has run away from his parents
and now to the police station is about to be carried
Let them know that they can have a clean slate
Restore their smiles and remove the pain
I pray dear Lord for your amazing grace
To fall afresh on their hearts and brighten their faces

Lord help them realize that the true joys in life
don't get you high for awhile
They thrive in your mind and always make you smile
Lord this is a prayer for the cold, lonely, and scolded
the high school kid who is trying to fit the molding
the man who can not handle the conflicts unfolding
the woman who is crying and has no shoulders to hold her
Lord let them know that with you they have a home
because your arms are large enough to hold them all
If only they would hear your voice calling

there is a helping hand outstretched
to those who are weak
living water for those who dive to the bot-
tom of bottles every week

Bless those who now will fill their veins with drugs
or search for love in nights of lust
Lord show them so they may know
that there is something greater
than all the acid, weed, and methamphetamines
greater than vodka shooters, hypnotic, and Hennessey
greater than Bentleys, beamers, Mercedes, and Ferraris,
Lord bless them with a mind of peace

Because Lord you know when the crack high crashes
we are still afflicted and the origi-
nal sickness is still in existence
and on top of those conflicts we now add addictions
You know that when we wake up in the sheets all alone
and that man or woman has gone home
there is still an emptiness and a night
of indulgence won't fill it
Because we can be blessed with money
and we will buy all of the things we want

But no amount of money can change
the results on a medical chart
Wealth can't buy health, and death
doesn't accept checks
because when our time comes,
God, you are not worried about our credit

You are looking at our souls and how we lived our lives
We can run and duck from many things
but we cannot hide from You.
Lord lighten the path and turn our hearts to Christ
That we may know true joy in this life
Rest, rule, and abide forever by our sides
God, this is my prayer for the lost of mankind.

On the Corner

Her sister calls her filthy
her mother doesn't speak
Her father's jaw just drops to the tabletop
and her brother can't believe it
Her husband-to-be
requests his ring
and swiftly dismisses the possibility
that they will ever marry
she stands...
her only option is to leave

No one follows her
she walks alone
Broken—she goes back

to those paying patrons
that she gave
her most precious possession
Allowing them to enter her and exit
doing as they pleased in between

Asking a price for her pleasure
a cost for her company
Day after day, she walks the block
and seeing her I wonder...

What amount of money
could buy back her dignity
This lady of the evening
has no identity
She has no present or past
no history or family
similar to a taxi cab
that you buy for a ride
and leave for the next guy
She's seen not as a person
but most as a service
She has been reduced to less than human
and seems oblivious to it

Refusing the reality
that she is a whore
and that someone may never again
view her as anything more
I want to give it back to her

all that she has lost
all that she has given away
all that was taken
But I can't do that
I can only forget
that it ever happened

And take her for who she is
and give not one thought to who she was
care not what she did
but only what she does
Remind her that she's worth it
and worthy of so much more
She has a future
because God and I don't care
what happened before
She can be born again
she can have a new life
she can shake off the darkness
and walk in a new light
Leave the world behind
and regain her self-respect
look into the mirror
and smile at her reflection

Nine Eleven

Father in Heaven
Today is September 11
and I ask today for some very special blessings
on New York City and Washington, DC
on that town in Pennsylvania
and the families of the fallen on United Flight 93
I pray for the lifting of spirits for
those who have suffered loss
And provision for the families
Now struggling with living costs
Because when the dust settled, it was not about planes
Buildings, or box-cutter blades,
Oil, politics, Al-Qaeda or the United States
After the calming of the frenzied media
We finally start to remember the people
Yes, there were analysts and investors
Brokers and janitors and staff
But God I'm not talking about what they did
I'm talking about more than that
They were sons and daughters, moms and dads

I pray that we would remember the people
Instead of getting lost in the aftermath of an attack
Be with the motherless child that doesn't understand
And that mother that must show
her son how to be a man
That father who doesn't have his daughter anymore
That broken family that doesn't know what's in store
I ask that you would heal wounds dear God
And sew lives back together
And you promised if we pray in faith
You will bless us says Matthew 7
So those who seek peace,
Father I pray that they would find it
And those who can't forgive
I pray that they wouldn't deny it
Father, last but not least,
I praise and thank you for those lives saved
For those lights in this world that were not taken
I also thank you for those who were called home
And will forever remember the light that they gave us
Father send your spirit forever with us to dwell
and hold us close when waves of pain swell

Amen

You Can't Run

You think no one's chasing you
so you do not run
you think the problem is gone
because when you turn—there is no one
But out of the darkness
some distance in front
streetlight casts a shadow
and there is someone
The silhouette of a figure
possessing no face
Slowly coming towards you
as if to explore you
Frozen by fear, you do not move
but meet the brute
who is now before you
Instead of retreating again
you clench your fists to react
but the figure only raises its hands
to remove a mask
And as you stand before the darkness

who in your mind was someone else
you quickly stand to realize
that before you stands yourself

Too Much

I'm being pulled in too many directions
I feel as if I'm doing too much
voices swirl about me
left and right, back and front
My soul is weary, my mind needs to rest
so many opportunities
too much for me to digest
I feel that my input is vital
so I offer no objections
Everyone has advice
there is no limit to suggestions

I have been blessed with abilities
and have an abundance of skill
so how can I choose a single task
where my emptiness will be filled
There is work to be done
chores to be performed
whirling about my head
like a raging sandstorm

Lord guide my steps
help me make the right choices
open my ears
that I may discern the voices

Real Dreams

I had a dream
but not like Martin Luther King
This was not a struggle for humanity
but a battle for me
Now for those who don't know
exactly what the rapture is
It's when God comes to claim His own
and like a thief in the night,
comes the Lord Jesus Christ
to take His saved ones home

So there I stood
in my country home,
in front of the stove

with my mother, sister, and brother
talking about the events of the day
not knowing that my God was coming

I turned my back
and in a flash
they were there no more
three living forms
were now three piles of clothes
folded on the floor

Now it's not like the pain
of not getting picked in fifth grade gym
or being cut from the basketball team
because your jump shot doesn't fall
It was a pain that was so deep,
because it wasn't the coach or your best friend, Jimmy
who looked over you…
it was God who looked at your soul
and He hadn't chosen you

Now I took inventory of church services I had been in,
prayers I had prayed, all the church plays
and the parts I played… played, played, played…
what about that girl I played when in bed we lay
and she stopped me from going all the way…
when I'm supposed to be a man of God,
or is that just what I portray…

Portrayed a speaker, weaving fine words
moving crowds to their feet …
then that same tongue spinning words
that stung minds and hearts
with words that start with F and end in UCK.

What about all those times,
people stood on the corners with no money,
and I pretended I didn't have any either …
because I thought he was just gonna drink or buy reefer
When it didn't matter because that little gift
and a God bless might change his existence,
life path, and final place in eternity

I chose to please myself—man …
and not take a stand—
to be exactly what the world wanted me to be
instead of what God made me to be …
Therefore because in those moments
I was ashamed of Him
In that moment, He was ashamed of me …
In one moment, that lack of motion on my part
was a culmination of the lack of changes
my life was not willing to make …

God chose to show me, to warn me ...
that when that day comes
He wasn't going to take me ...
that when His Son cracked that east sky
I was going to say goodbye to all the Christians

I thought I was a part of ...

Two Fathers

Father I

Positive or negative
plus or minus
white or striped?

Overtaken by nervousness
my hands tremble
and my palms sweat
Her back shields
the results from my eyes
her back, the barrier

The clock ticks,
m e a s u r i n g t h e l o n g e s t 9 0 s e c o n d s
of my existence

She turns to me....
I am to be a father.

A father—me
a boy myself, not yet a man
but old enough to make one
seventeen years old
but not grown enough to raise one

God why?
I used all methods of protection
pills and contraception
but still she stands before me pregnant

I have my whole life Lord
I have not begun to live
I have not seen the world
and now I will have a kid

Who knew I'd be contemplating these options
choosing between colleges, then abortion or adoption
going from job fair to day cares, diapers and high chairs
a life beginning and ending with high school
because of tiny spoons filled with baby food
Mother, Father, and Father God
I know not what to do,

Lord Jesus, I need
strength and guidance from you.

Father II

Positive or negative
plus or minus
white or striped?

Overtaken by nervousness
my hands tremble
and my palms sweat
Her back shields
the results from my eyes
her back, the barrier

The clock ticks,
m e a s u r i n g t h e l o n g e s t 9 0 s e c o n d s
of my existence

She turns to me....
                    I am not to be a father

A father, so long we had tried with no success
in vitro fertilization and new medical practices
and here we stand again, unsuccessful

A boy or girl,
Dear God, I care not which
Oh Lord, my child, our child
just one blessed gift

Lord I ask you for a miracle
a child to call my own
a son or daughter to raise
in a good and Godly home

Peewee practices or dance classes to attend
Lord I want the chance to be PTA president
Lord Jesus please, I just want to be a parent
to give a son my name, or a daughter away in marriage

Lord I ask you for a boy
and I will name him John,
for his name means nothing less
than a gift from God
or Lord, a girl

and I will call her Heaven
for I would know she was an angel
sent directly from your presence

Father I stretch my hands to thee
Jesus please bless me ...

with a child

So Heavy

He carries the lives
of lost loved ones
like caskets stacked on his back
Shoulders low
weighed down
by the figures in his past
Time is forever going forward
but he is forever looking back
At what once was
at what could have been
staring over his shoulder
at the beginning of his journey
constantly considering what
he could have done differently

When will he turn
avert his gaze from before
to concentrate on the future
and those things he can change
I know not the minute,

not the hour, nor the day
that he will look up
and show us his face
But I pray that day comes
before he collapses under life's weight

Standing on the Promises

With two feet firmly
on the promises of God
He stands—
rooted in his faith
The stains of life washed away
cleansed of a marred existence
smiling to himself
because of the path he has chosen
He would not change it for the world

But then the storms of life
grow stronger
and the periods of pain
last much longer
His body now wrapped in illness
his heart still sings the same song
Amazing is that grace
that saved a wretch like me

I once was lost but now I'm found
I was blind but now I see

With slow hands and closed eyes
he turns to Habakkuk 3
and his cracking voice reads three verses—
his personal testimony:

Although the fig tree shall not blossom,
neither shall fruit be in the vines;
the labour of the olive shall fail,
and the fields shall yield no meat;
the flock shall be cut off from the fold,
and there shall be no herd in the stalls:
[18] Yet I will rejoice in the Lord,
I will joy in the God of my salvation.
[19] The Lord God is my strength,
and he will make my feet like hinds' feet,
and he will make me to walk upon my high hills.

My Name Is...

This is our epigraph
See I was walking to classes, AKA my own
road to Damascus, past St. Paul's Chapel
Down the red brick paths to elevate my edu-
cated status when I felt it.

Part of my memory had gangrene so I cut
it off so the rest of me could live.
I buried the pieces deep inside myself
... and life's floodwaters washed me back to my surface.
I looked at me who had been forgot-
ten and began to write my story
                                        My name is Simon

Black, Sudanese, Christian
An identity that the world has
labeled "permanent victim"
An identity that is invisible
An identity millions strong but the first
world has yet to acknowledge

My name is Simon

But like a tree planted by the river Nile, I stand
More than a man—a faith-filled sur-
vivor of slavery for 4,028 days
My name is Simon

But my name is also Grace
Black, female, Ugandan
Ripe and available for the sex trade
Kidnapped from school, taken by the LRA
My name is Grace.

My life was taken once by rape, twice by thirst
Both times soldiers covered me with dirt
But my Savior sent me back to this Earth
Because in me He had begun a good work.
Two hundred days and I escaped, now
standing here in the United States
My name is Grace.

My name is also Soon He
Young, female, North Korean
Sold into China, where they traffic my humanity

promising me food if I would just cross the border
sold for three hundred dollars, then cleaned and sorted
by eye color, chest size, overall body shape

My name is Toko Tamita—taken in Cambodia
My name is Jacob from the UK, Alejandro
from El Salvador, Preeti in Calcutta,
All free in the United States.
I am free but former slave, now open-
ing my eyes I remember me
I have 800,000 names behind my 800,000 faces
with 800,000 different testimo-
nies of how my life was taken
but you are one ... one with power, one with voice
you are one who can now make a choice
to make sure that I have the chance
to see my home again ...

Change of Plans

Dear Mom and Dad,

I am standing on the threshold of who I want to be looking back at who I am, and wondering why I didn't see this before.

They say that hindsight is 20/20, then my foresight must have been like 50/100 and my insight like a blind man fondling the darkness for a light switch in a room with no walls.

Because when I took this path I thought I was taking route progress. I assumed I was going down the road that was the best by taking the track more traveled but instead jumped on train lack of self-respect, ended up in distress, depressed and signaling SOS to strangers in all directions.

I don't want to be a doctor, a lawyer, or bite my nails in an office. I want to heal heart wounds with my words, prosecute politicians with my pen, and invest in audiences willing to listen to a college graduate who wanted so bad to drop out but couldn't because he knew the true value of an education.

I'm changing my major from Biology pre-med to

major in life with a double-concentration in success and excellence. My courses include three semesters of charity, two courses on good will towards man, and a required seminar on increasing my measure of faith.

My thesis proves man must know his past before he understands his present or comprehends his future and I live out my Savior's motto that to whom much is given, much more is required. I don't see life like it is, I close my eyes and envision how it could be and slave to make my dreams a reality. I hope you love me for trying to make this world a better place for the next generation and I promise your hard-earned money is not wasted. My words are all I have so I hope you take them and save them in that special place that expectation can't get to. I met God and now I have to live like I know who He is.

Insight Is Ageless

The fear of the Lord is the beginning of wisdom; all
who follow his precepts have good understanding.

Psalm 111:10 (NIV)

No Interference

Let me for a moment forget
that I am a US citizen
Have never been blitzed by the media
or heard the promises of politicians
Seldom seen a GQ or Cosmo
and never viewed television shows
Turned deaf ears to MTV
and only looked inside myself
for the image of me
Because I cannot let popular opinion
compromise my convictions
or when I reach crossroads
let voter's polls dictate which way I go
Society cannot influence all of my decisions
Because my shoulders are the only shoulders
to bear the weight of the consequences
Because those same ones advising
will judge my guilt or innocence
and no matter what I do
there is no pleasing all of them

so I must discern what is right in my mind
Study to show myself approved
right dividing the word of truth
because the choice has always been mine
and the time is now to choose.

Look Deeper

When you look at a pencil,
what do you see?
just a cylinder of lead and graphite
or a symbol of endless possibilities

When you look at a glass of water
what do you really see?
just another cup of H_2O,
or a ripened piece of the sea
When you look at a television
what is it that you see
just another picture on the screen
or do you view the marvelous configuration
of the red, blue, and green light beams

When you look at an object,
whatever it may be
Don't admire the cover, look deep
because it is probably much more than it seems

The Balance

Two hands can give life
or two hands can take it away
two hands have the power
to destroy or to create
Joined with two strong arms
two hands can heal or harm
Combined with a discerning mind
choices are made between right and wrong
Two seeing eyes, act as simple guides
trying to help the mind discern darkness and light
Two stepping feet, follow forked paths
moved by two legs away from the past
Of each finger there are also two
cheeks, knees, nipples, and nostrils too
every digit, having a yin and a yang
keeping the balance true

They Made Me

So many things go wrong each day
leave me speechless, nothing to say
The whole world stares into my face
but they do not see what is taking place
An invisible wall that cannot be found.
not seen, not heard, like invisible ultrasound
This act I've played since an early age
Everyday I wake, I take the stage
I stand there, and people gaze
I look around and search for escape
Maybe a trap door, through which I can slip
forget what is normal, dismiss the script
Death to these images that I have thought
Death to these scenes that I have seen
I refuse to play this part
Extinguish these internal embers
erase my memory, I don't want to remember
replace with the pureness,
of a first snow in December
lift my spirits, for they fall like timber

But if my memory ceases to be
won't that mean the end of me
because with all my experiences
goes my personality
because all of these trials
in turn made me
Every success, every failure
every occurrence, each event
every person I have passed
every person I have met
every acquaintance, every friend
All of the places I have gone
everywhere that I have been
everything I ever did
every good deed and every sin
these things I am a product of
my being a direct result
all of these things made me
my life form, the clay they sculpted.

Rain

The animals have gone quiet
and the birds have ceased to sing
giving the Earth peace
as it prepares to drink
the silence is broken
by the pitter patter of droplets
as the dropping water spatters
and fills the earth's thirsty pockets
First————————slow
almost a quiet snapping sound
Then the pace is quickened
and rain swiftly hits the ground
With the rustling of leaves
and the wind's whirring whistle
this language of nature is created
as the sounds create a mixture
As it strikes my ears
I can hear nature speak
a conversation between the Earth and sky
through water, wind, and leaves

Slowly the wind blows
and the water flows and soaks
until it has quenched the soil
and the clouds have returned home

Such Is Life

Such is life
the positive backspins
emotional whirlwinds
and physical dispositions

Such is this existence
the sorry excuses
and excessive individuals
who lead lacking
and illustrious lives

Such is this globe
a circular mold
folded to fit into
the theorems and laws
of an overbearing man

Such is this universe
cursed by its inhabitants
and blessed by those
who stand beside them

Positive

My mind lies in rewind
remembering events of yesterday
and I allow it to go there
to go there—to stay there
to become so completely rapt in there
that I am no longer here
Home where all was well
Home where I lost my shell
Home where the outside of me
was the inside of me
and world embraced all of me

Home …

Where the tea is sweet
and the biscuits come with gravy
and men always hold the doors for ladies

Home…
Where the people are polite
where you can walk the streets at night
and the stars are not blotted by street lights

My brain remains in replay
remembering events of before
and I let myself be lost in them
let myself need, let myself breathe
let myself be on the outside
what the inside is of me
Let myself be

The man who says *yes ma'am* and please
goes to church on Sunday and is not ashamed of
Christianity
does not indulge in ignorance and cyclic vanity
and only wishes to uplift humanity

Home is where I left a piece
Home is where I wish to be
Home—that place I only see in my dreams
as I lay in the city that never sleeps

But before tears of reminiscing rush down my cheeks
They are dried by echoes of early teachings
One must realize that you can not replay
but only review in an attempt to recreate
those cherished yesterdays
those treasured yestermoments
that we wish to rendezvous with
Those perfect stints of yesterminutes
that we wish to deja vu with

We must learn from the past
if we wish or wish not to renew it
because the past has already been
and we can only review it
Wait—wait
pause—
rewind—
then press play—
You can only review to recreate
yes—it is true
the future is before your face and there is no going back
to all that has taken place

Learn from the past
live for the now
and carry all into the future.

Sun and Moon

As the sun rises
so does the sun set
given up in the east
and swallowed by the west
Like an experienced actor
waiting for the perfect cue
the sun falls down
and so rises the moon
every day—every night
This cycle continues
between the sun and the moon
up and down, up and down
dancing to a silent tune

Shooting Star

Swimming through a black sea
at possibly thousands of degrees
A shooting star goes across the sky
a flaming piece of space debris
Like a fallen angel it plummets to Earth
leaving a fiery trail across the heavens
as a mother calls for her children
our gaze this wonder beckons
Followed by eyes around the globe
on the backs of porches or on top homes
we stare in awe at nature's beauty
though this spectacle's origin, is unknown
And before this opportunity is missed
an age old tradition is practiced
From that front door or that bedroom window
everyone pauses to make a wish

Business as Usual

My brother's right arm is a little bit longer than his left
because one day in DC,
a fall caused his clavicle and scapula to separate.
He walked up to my mom, arm limp,
simple and pleading for Momma's assistance
I wish it were true about a mother's kiss—

She wrapped him in her arms
and then wrapped his arm
in a towel.
Then taking an iron
wrapped it and his arm in a diaper -
turned the dial to "low"
gave him a pillow
and on the sofa he sat for two and a half weeks

My brother's right arm is a little bit longer than his left.
…
I live in Brodnax, but I was born
in Fairfax, suburban DC

my brother went to TJ, best pub-
lic school in the country
but he had no blue cross or blue shield and mom, her
wallet could not yield the dollars to the hospital
So she became surgeon, nurse, bed atten-
dant, and machine—made
iron, towel, diaper—her ingredients for healing
and did her best to make her son's pain disappear
because that is what you do when
you have no insurance.

My momma is a teacher, not kindergarten, but Pre-K.
and I read stories to a girl named Alice at
recess because she can't run and play
she looks up at me, thinning hair and tired eyes
wanting to climb the monkey bars, or just go outside
but her white blood cells are wag-
ing war against her body—
and for the first time I saw what leukemia looked like

Five thousand people in my town, 12,000 in my county
and every singer and artist gathered their talent
to help raise money for treatment for Alice.
Maybe a song, a poem, or a personal testimony

would drown out the voice of a com-
pany that says her life isn't worth it
Maybe seeing all of us will make it eas-
ier when she closes her eyes
maybe memories of our songs will
make it easier when she dies
because that is what you do when
you have no insurance

Healthcare is the topic but welfare is the issue
as the individual disappears and
is replaced with an issue
as his face will disappear and be replaced with an issue
as her name will disappear and be
renamed with an issue
as her memory will be here and we will debate an issue

Conditions show up on statistics, but
my brother's name will not
as board members debate econom-
ics, Alice's heart will stop
as policy makers form commit-
tees, hospital doors will lock

as time forges forward, the balance shifts
from the haves to have-nots

There are people broken with cabinets full of splints
there are people sick with closets full of medicine
This system has a sickness and maybe it has no policy
as I pen this poem my own thought
processes stop me ...

For a moment I thought hospi-
tals were for helping people
I forgot in America it's just a business

Anger Consumed Me

I hear verbs from behind curtains
lurking in the depths but never emerging
cowards cowering behind veils of jealousy
spewing words, saying nothing
but still the sound is loud and bellowing
My wish is my will to strangle them
vanish into the darkness and vanquish them
inflict forceful recourse upon the source
violently silence those vocal cords
score tremendous, horrendous gore
worthy of entry into the horror section
at the local movie store
I move forward away from the noise not towards
because to face this foe, my status would be lowered
But still I hear the flapping tongue
my ears capture the smacking gums
I can no longer take it, I must not run
I possess no more patience, my nerves are done
My breaking point has been reached
I turn and unleash the beast within me

my fury is released until quiet peace is reached
…
…
…
Now I sit behind these bars
for allowing anger to consume my heart

Forgive Me

Because everything has been done
there is nothing left for me to do
There is nothing left for me to say
because words can't heal wounds
I cannot reverse the hands of time
nor in the sands can I remove the lines
Upon you—there is nothing I could bestow
to reflect the regret that is in my soul
no gesture, no action, could accurately show
the sadness inside me—the pain, the sorrow
From the bottom of my heart I do repent
my entire being is engulfed in torment
my mind is consumed by constant resentment
take the meaning of these words to the fullest extent
From the depths of my soul I do apologize
You could not count the tears I have cried
My remorsefulness you could not assess
so at this moment, I ask your forgiveness

Insight Is Ageless

Age is nothing but a number
a measure of the days that we rise and slumber
a sum of the seasons that we have seen
the autumns, the winters,
the springs and the summers
but who says that adulthood is true maturity
I challenge the majority go against seniority
because I refuse to have society score me
Human time is not a true measurement
of the growth of the human mind
sundials measure days and nights
but not the enlightenment of life
Wisdom within cannot be standardized
because tests and time are only calculations
they are truly undefined
Because insight is ageless
knowledge is faceless
those who do not respect the young
are truly brainless
but those accepting changes

are truly dangerous
for knowledge is power
the possibilities nameless
Destined for greatness
success no longer tasteless
They say close but no cigar
but with wisdom your mind attains it
so don't quote what is to be known
from graphs of bars
and charts that flow
for it is not from strokes of chalk
and copied notes
that true knowledge transpires and is truly known
But it is that wisdom which walks
without height nor width
is plainly before us and in our mind just fits
because it is common sense that is true intelligence
a gift from God that is freely given.

My Boots

The soles are low and worn and the laces are faded from their original shade of iron, rubbed by the bottoms of blue pantlegs and pavement that turned to dirt and gravel too quickly. These are the boots I wear. Those were the boots I wore. These boots are those boots that took me from the tobacco fields in Brodnax, past the train tracks of LaCrosse, to the locker rooms in South Hill where I went to school at Park View. These boots took me home and to and fro and wherever I go I will carry them because they carried me. They traveled to New York City but have never touched my feet because in their present state they remind me of where I came from and show me where I belong. These were the boots that stepped in horse shit on hot summers on Gene Kennedy's farm. These were the boots that pushed John Deere pedals when I crisscrossed my Uncle Marvin's lawn. These boots are signals of my history and if I sit quietly I can hear them stepping the rhythm of hip-hop and gospel, jazz, and bluegrass on the way to the church cemetery because I want to see the deacons from before my time. These were my boots. Brown. Size 13. Timberland. My boots.

River of Currency

I'm writing this poem for my momma
the public school teacher in LaCrosse, Virginia,
who chose to reach kids, teach kids,
hold kids and mold kids into productive members
of a broken society while surviving on a sal-
ary below the line of poverty

I'm inscribing these lines for the
Seventeen students at UVA who were
arrested for protesting for a living wage
not for themselves but for the work-
ers that clean their dormitories
workers can't afford to live in the same place
when they work at the richest school in the state
All they are asking for is 10.72
that's ten dollars and seventy-two cents
so that after taxes
they can barely break 20,000

I'm writing this poem for that dude
in the Merrill Lynch mailroom
who knows he's bringing home
fifty times less than the reigning CEO
I'm writing because there is a guy riding a bike
right now trying to get that Chinese food to
the right place in less than fifteen minutes
a pregnant woman ringing groceries as fast as she can
because she has no money for a medical plan
the man throwing dough to make your personal pan
I'm writing to give a voice to the American worker
who is being broken and bent over by
the forever responsible man

I'm writing this poem
because capitalistic individualism is kill-
ing individuals with minimum capital
as the individual only seeks to maximize his capital,
killing individuals less fortunate than himself...

I'm writing because I'm upset with our
supposedly elected president
who looks down on a grossly misrepre-
sented senate and house of representatives

to raise his salary from two hundred and
fifty to four hundred thousand

Capitalism is cracking crippling whips on the back of
our working class but we've been beaten for so long, we
are immune and walking wounded … swept up in an
invisible river bigger than the Mississippi, slicker than
the Harlem and less swimmable than the Hudson …

This is the river of currency
and currently the current is so strong
that the working class is riding the riptide
far out into sea, too far to see land
but hoping that if we keep working some-
day we'll reach the beach …

I'm writing this poem, and I'll keep writing this
poem, binding and refining the lines in this poem
until my momma can teach kids to read and be
able afford her mortgage, eat out every once in
a while and drive the car she'd like to work.

I'm Sorry Anna Nicole

I step up to a magazine stand and it's like stepping
up to an auction block and sex is for sale
as I see the bodies of females on display
for *my trying not to look like I'm viewing pleasure . . .*
and I think to myself, which one is worse
a burka or bulimia?
Ladies, "Free yourselves, so we can buy you,
don't worry about your value,
because we will define you"
because happenings minus the facts
equals the news for us
and news equals the truth for us
so Anna Nicole must have died from an overdose . . .

But I know that there's a thin line
between tight and too small
so pornography is just prostitution with taxes
and the fact is Anna Nicole lost her
power of definition and it killed her
She became a commodity, a novelty

and it really starts to bother me as I think
of how brothers under covers, went to
the gutter and had her for $2.99

So this is my apology because I was one of them
a letter asking forgiveness from the hearts of all women

Dear Anna Nicole, Jenna Jameson,
and those vivid video vixens
Gianna Michaels, those playmates in penthouse
and those pictures on the Internet that
have no names just descriptions
I wish I could write you a check and
give you back what I took
give you a DVD or a magazine
to upload your self worth, download your dignity,
read your truth or just see what you're really worth
because I witnessed images that I didn't have a right to
and I can't erase my memory so I have to write you
and apologize for taking some-
thing that I paid for a price
but no matter how high, should have never been mine

I realized something standing on the cor-
ner of Broadway and 116th
as I saw fifty-seven magazines and women
covered covers of fifty-three
that these weren't just bodies, they were sis-
ters, daughters, and mothers
and it was my call to be the best hus-
band, son, and brother

Now with a changed heart trying to
change my mind and my desires
Anna Nicole makes me worry but
the unnamed make me cry
because how many girls have died or been hospitalized
from not eating trying to be the right size
How many pills have been popped, and how
many drips of blood have been dropped
onto bathroom floors, behind dorm room
doors and those other doors with locks
on the opposite sides of cell blocks

When will we wake up and realize we're
raising a generation of *prostitots*
kids that know how to suck and
f—k before they know love
know multiple positions before they know long division
and the minority becomes those who
aren't sexual assault victims

This is for Denise laying down in front of
her webcam and following directions
the wife who just found her hus-
band's private pleasure collection
the girl at the bus stop who has just been molested
the lady walking the street followed
by cat-calls and craned necks

I'm sorry and that's all that I can say…
but I promise when I have a son,
I'll raise him to respect you
and if my poems were bricks, I'd build
word walls to protect you
from males not worthy to hold the title of man.

Sisters and mothers, I'm sorry…
Husbands, sons, and brothers please pick up your bats
because the women of this world
are waiting for us to step up.

Invisible Children

I'm breathing in the last breathes of the Acholi
running with Jacob as he flees Joseph Coney
bleeding, wheezing, maimed, and beaten
wheezing I'm bleeding, blameless but beaten
beaten and bleeding, coughing and wheezing
breathing in the last of the Acholi
See Jacob—he is part of the Acholi Tribe
and he is just one invisible child
a faceless name with forty thousand others just like him
a nameless face as you see him on adver-
tisements ... See Jacob
He walks eight miles looking back all the while
because another child soldier could attack and kidnap
and he will be forced to trade his backpack
for an AK-47 and an army knapsack

Fear is the rebels' main weapon
and they spread death like an infection
so children are paralyzed, no threat of an insurrection
Ages eight to fourteen, boys are given guns
and girls are simply given to someone

I close my eyes and in the streets I am sleeping
trying to wake up from this dream
I can't believe this is happening to me …
                                    I wake up
but Jacob never does
because this nightmare is his lifemare
that I can't dream through, that I can't sleep through
but he walks through, talks through,
and praises God all through

I am looking at a blank page
trying to paint the faces of invisible individuals
with my words
Trying to capture a reality
that my mind can't grasp with a pen and a pad
I'm trying to be that poet that writes that poem
that actually does this story justice
But I've seen that documentary

not once, not twice, but nine times times three
and it's on permanent repeat in my mind's TV
I hear Jacob saying I would rather be dead
see a crying priest draw a cross
from his heart to his head
see an entire country drowning in bloodshed
I don't want to see another *Hotel Rwanda*
I don't want to see another swollen belly from Somalia
I don't want to see another photo from the Congo
I don't want to see these invisible children so I don't.

They are invisible to me, invisible to us
invisible to everyone because we've intentionally chosen
not to acknowledge their humanity

Tony said "Don't forget about me,
don't forget about me."
Lock me in the vaults of your memory
replay my face every day and remember me
                                    remember me

I am looking at a blank page filled with words
unworthy to tell Jacob's story
but I kept my promise that I took
when I walked with him when I talked with him
"Don't forget me," Tony said—and I can't
because they are the only things that I remember

War

War seems to be when two sides cease to speak
refuse to reconcile and choose violence instead of peace
Now it is said there is a time for war
and a season for peace
Wisdom written in the words of Ecclesiastes
but it would seem to me
that alternative agendas have determined the need
Adversaries of ideals lift their pens from peace treaties
and hastily place them on war decrees
Diplomats back away from tables of communication
and Generals rush to war rooms to replace them
Governments start trading books for bombs
the light of education dims and ignites
the flame of nationalism
Media then fans the flames
masking the factual and bending the actual
until we are no longer sure of reality
only sure of many maladies
for which we have no cure

All this while saying – the end justifies the means
but never asking the question
where's your end point
if you were wrong from the beginning

If we do not learn from the past
we are destined to repeat it
where will we be in thirty years
just take a look at history

War is not numbers and figures
cannot be counted in millions and billions
but in currency of lost eyes and lost limbs
crying wives and kids
empty tables with broken spirits
at Thanksgiving and Christmas
Count the armless and the quadriplegics
the scarred and those with bad dreams
Veterans commit seventeen suicides a week
is this what it costs to be free?

Decisions

We have to make some decisions
because there are racial divisions
Blacks and whites got a schism
some people call it racism
because the looks that are given
put us in awkward positions
from Minnesota to Mississippi
from LA to Virginia
But there's not a color limit
to this discriminate system
as many races, religions, political, and social positions
are cause for division
just relax and listen, close your eyes and envision

Catholicism versus Protestantism
prejudice held between Hindu, Muslim, and Jewish
tradition
malice mounted between Chinese and Koreans
Bad borders between Pakistanis and Indians

Friction with Israelis and Palestinians
and now the Lebanese and the Syrians
Rwandans, Ugandans, the Congolese, and Nigerians
the list of conflicts is as big as the world we are living
in but—
Hatred has never been the mission of any religion
so this tradition would certainly seem sacrilegious
because Jesus certainly teaches to love your neighbor as
yourself
and God is definitely blessing us and everybody else
so—
separate we can fall or together we can grow
because it's a cruel cold world when you walk through
it alone

These aren't black and white issues
these are wrong and right issues
and there is no reason for a human being to have to
argue his humanity.

We live in a supposedly postmodern world
that looks more medieval everyday
Our world is educated and ignorant
embracing and intolerant

wealthy but so unhealthy
so quick to raise money but so slow to begin helping

When will we lower our rifle scopes
and focus our microscopes
trade our bombs for books
change the world lens through which we look
and see people and not problems
see people—and not potential for profit
see people—and not obstacles
but see living, breathing, loving people

There is no first world or third world
because separation only means a worse world

This world is full of bold and soulful people
loud, outspoken people, some
supposedly holy rolling people
but also silent, quiet people, those
victim of violence people
emotion holding people, malnourished,
stomach-swollen people
This globe overflows with people
but our hearts and minds must stay open to all people

because we are all individuals but
we are all God's people

Unique and different in many different ways but
so much the same if only we could change just
open our eyes and read between the lines
and see the beauty that lies on the inside

Just Like You

Your mouth is full of empty speech
foul words painting a picture of your mentality
out of the abundance of the heart, the mouth speaks
so you bear your insides for all to see
Like a bloom-filled briar patch
you attract attention
but upon inspection
one finds it difficult to kick against the pricks
and leaves it in the same condition

You are resistant to progress
allergic to growth
Your development is non-existent
or so slow no one notices

Where is your ambition—
your thirst for independence
your want to make your words count for something
and not just crass sentences
displaying your mental limits

If not for you, then for your kids
for they more than anyone
see the life that you live
and you may be blind to them
but they see and want to be just like you

Just like their dad, their pop, their father
but you seem like you don't want to be bothered—
So you bow away from the ladder of responsibility

To Whom It May Concern:

I'm lost and I don't think I can find myself because I've searched where most people look and look my hands are empty. It's worse than trying to find a needle in a haystack—it's like trying to find your pin in a needle stack when all of them bear your name in languages you can't read. I look forward in my life and see roads, roads not taken, paths proven to fail, and roads that look okay as far as I can see but I stand still and still looking. I look behind me and there are fingers, fingers pointing and fingers poised to point in every direction with voices behind them saying *this is the right way*.

You turn your back and your spouse was only pretending to be happy when you worked those extra hours to buy that new Rover, when all she wanted was you. You missed it, and I don't want to imagine what it looked like when Jackie rode her bike without training wheels for the first time, or Justin made a man out of Play-Doh and said it was his daddy. I want to be the big man holding his wife's hand in the sketches filled in with Crayola colors and not a memory in a mind that does not want to remember. I want to be there. And you weren't. So I don't want to be like you.

Backwards

The privileged adorn the finest silk
beige as butter or white as milk
virtuous violet or mother of pearl
flaunting woven webbings
from worms in the third world
Society has lost its loyalty to origin
lost in progress, disregarding the story
labeled as history, when brought back is boring
repeating past mistakes while trying to move forward
Each of us crawled before we could walk
we babbled as brooks before we could talk
As a whole we marvel at inventions
forgetting a mind conjured that thought
Every bountiful harvest
had its beginnings as a seedless garden
farmers driving steel plows
tilling thirsty ground that hardened
Cereal is not spawned in box
nor are diamonds man-made rocks
grain is refined, then baked hot

and Africans gather pressurized knots
Today's minds are like septic lines
clogged with nonsense and lack of insight
an epidemic of ignorance
that is spreading like a snakebite
Infecting today's youth with a disease called stupidity
our vessels are more beautiful
but within they are more empty
Across classrooms, students look up with weary eyes
with gossip they are occupied,
to knowledge—access is denied
like a busy phone line
ridiculous inquisitions then arise
"Like, why do we need to learn about those guys
if they are old or they already died?"
Man, plant, and animal, did not burst into existence
nor is anything given—created in an instant
So when history is reading, we all must listen
for precedents possess the pieces we are missing

Bang

Lingering sadness
a tragedy remembered
as a flame is extinguished
and soiled are the embers
All desires lost
all hopes cast away
only the innocence remains
before this life's song
has reached its first refrain
This sequence continues
as the moon waxes and wanes
This episode begins
every time a child is slain

The Wind of the World

The wind of this world
is taking my closest friends
snatching my peers
and engaging my kin
Whisking them away
down a road to destruction
that I can see, but to speak
is a futile function
For I am on the other side
flashing
flashing
flashing
my guiding light
but it seems like
I am sending *s m o k e* signals
up into the darkness of night
For they cannot
see me
or they choose not to acknowledge
so I watch my loved ones
be abolished by the darkness

Tool Box

There is a wooden box in the back corner of my Mom's closet where she keeps her tools. I remember when that wooden box was just wooden blocks in a shop class that taught boys to be men, manhood measured by what you could fix. The notches were done by hand with a half-inch chisel and a rubber hammer so you didn't damage the handle or your hands.

I modeled it after the one my Granddaddy made, the one that my real dad had taken. The daughter in my mom wanted it back but the ex-wife in her wouldn't let her ask—so being the man in the middle I made her one. Physically three sliced pine blocks replace one pine box, but closing my eyes I see so much more is here. This is for the lady that hasn't had a pair of shoes where hers were the first feet in them for more than fifteen years. This is for the momma that claims more kids than her own and has forever welcome hinges on her front door and folding chairs by the dinner table. This box is for my mom to put her tools in. Those tools that no one else gets to use because she mends herself with them. This box is my mom's; this box is no one else's.

Take Me To a Place

I am cursed
and I am blessed
I am the worst
and I am the best
It all depends
on the heart behind the eyes
that behold my flesh

Take me to a place
where racism doesn't exist
and I am not judged
by the color of my skin
Just take me to a place
where I am not hated
simply because of the way God made me
You show me that place
and I will give my soul to go
because it seems there's no place like that on Earth
so heaven must be my goal

I am in a precarious position
as I attempt to deal with racism
because I cannot hate them
because they already hate me
and if I show hate towards them
then the prejudice will never end
Fighting fire with fire
only enlarges the blaze
So love is the only thing
that can extinguish this hate

Outside, Inside

He chops off your finger
you give him the whole hand
He takes all you have
and you scrounge to give him more
No good has he done you
but only good will you do him

The golden rule is displayed before my face everyday
and though I have a measure of faith, if smacked in the
face
will I offer up the counterpart
to welcome the pain

Momma, Momma, why do you do it
why don't you clean your house
This house is full of home
except for the shadow that lurks about

I yearn to get here, and then hate home
because on the outside it looks fine
but this fish is full of bones.

Peace From War

Missiles cut like knife blades through silence
Like whistling razor blades slic-
ing through the nighttime
In Baghdad, Gaza, Mogadishu …

Tangled towers of misunderstanding
Blown apart by bunker busters dropped by B-2s–
                  maybe now things will be mended

Because cotton surely grows from patches of cabbage
and beets are certainly picked from apple blossoms
Peace trees are surely the products from buds of war.

Millions

A million individuals
And twice million more feet
Pouring into subways
And crowding city streets
No faces familiar
Strangers never speak
Even more seldom
Do the same two people meet
Negative hospitality
Rarely hearing speech
Eyes neglecting contact
And no mouths move to greet
"Good morning, how are you?"
ears anxious for reply
Ears left eternally waiting
As the person passes by

This cycle of silence continues
Day in and day out
In the east and in the west
From the north to the south
For everyone is afraid
Of whom they do not know

Touch of Class

She sits in a swivel chair
with a smile on her face
as the hair falls away
and her new look is created
Upon the stylist's completion
he hands her a looking glass
and she examines the lady gazing back
Her anticipation turns to elation
as she loves what he has done
the mirror displays the beauty
held within her all along

Day after day, week after week
the routine is repeated
as barbers and beauticians
don't just change the looks of people
But lift levels of self-confidence
as they edge up hair lines
and ignite the spirits of uniqueness
with each highlight and style

There is something special
about a shape-up
something refreshing
about a haircut
that puts new pep in your step
new light in your eyes
Because it's not just a change in your appearance
There is a change on the inside

The Painter

He captures the essence
of objects, people, places—all
and tries to commit them to canvas

As if a flower has
been planted, blossomed, and died
before anyone took notice
He paints the petals, stem, and pollen
in an effort to give us that lotus

To give us what we saw, see
or just missed—in its entirety
it is his gift, privilege, and duty
Why is no longer a mystery

He must dab and stroke
stroke and dab
passing forth and back
from canvas to pallet
in a talent filled passion
to take and place what's in his mind
on a surface for all to see

I Used To

I used to love to eat the unbaked dough of my momma's rolls. Soft and sweet, I was not supposed to eat—but I did, secretly. I got my fingers smacked because my momma comes back and what had risen is now flat.

Yeah.

I used to love to eat the unbaked dough of my momma's rolls. I used to love to play basketball on the monkey bars and toss the football on the seesaw. There were too many kids for this schoolyard and kickball always went too far, but I didn't know what overcrowded meant so I just thought it was cool to have my friends all in one place.

I used to love Hannah Ramsey, pigtails in her 49ers jacket, queen of the fifth grade. She stole my heart like my fudge round from my lunch box and the next day I gave her a ring-pop and you couldn't tell me that we weren't meant to be.

I used to love Sundays because the Richmond Times Dispatch was fat and in the middle was what Charlie Brown, Lucy, Snoopy, Archie, Katy Keene, and Garfield and Odie were doing this week—that was news; and church meant if I sat through service quietly I could get extra fried chicken to go with my extra collard greens and macaroni and cheese and slice of apple pie washed down by sweet tea—that was the heaven in my mind.

I used to love the government because I was the only one that could sing "My Country Tis of Thee" in the right key and smile because my brother was a sailor in the navy. I watched jets go zoooooom, thought guns were *so* cool, and knew my momma should be president.

I remember the day she said "Yousta-beez" don't make honey.

Crossing That River

The darkness descended
and I felt the world
    fall
        from
            me
            Slowly I sank
            into nothingness
            Then a warmness
            a welcome warmness
            that wholly embraced me
            as a blanket of fleece
            saving me from the coldness with out
            but also with in
            This peace was complete
            no pieces of tranquility
            no shards of bliss
            but all senses of fullness fulfilled

Love and Loneliness

And now these three remain: faith, hope and love. But the greatest of these is love.

- 1 Corinthians 13:13

Smile

I place the poem in her palms
and her eyes peer at its pages
her lips mimicking the phrases
as the emotions reflect on her face

Eyes that once slept on the page
now sleep upon me
her lips part ways
and she slowly lifts her cheeks

Instantly I was inspired
sparked within me
was a creative fire
for the breath of my soul
birthed a smile

The words, this work
for no one but you
I create, I form
to free the smile in you

True Beauty

True beauty is deep within
inside the heart
beneath the skin
An orb of exquisiteness
confined behind the eyes
released in words and actions
conjured by a thoughtful mind
Tasks forever performed
with precision and grace
bringing a sense of fullness
to all empty space
Before you, the depths of beauty
my mind could not fathom
but now that I am with you
I no longer have to imagine

Love and Loneliness

If love is the strongest emotion in existence
then loneliness is the strongest state of mind
different in the thoughts they produce
but both alike in the power they find

You do not learn to appreciate love
until that love is lost
and when you feel loneliness
you realize that love was worth the cost

Loneliness is the bottom of the barrel
and love is at the top looking up
Love would be the grape, ripe on the vine
and loneliness would be the grape crushed

Love is having a beautiful day
even when the sun does not shine
and loneliness is having a frown on your face
when there is not a cloud in the sky

Only when you live through a drought
can you appreciate the rain from above
only when you experience loneliness
can you grasp the essence of love

With No Love

If we did not take the risk to love
dare our hearts to feel
our lives would be barren
sparse as winter fields
For if we did not love
no love would we receive
led by an assuming mind
false peace would be believed
For without love,
life is an open sheath,
nothing on Earth can fill you
no matter the blade you keep
For without love
no one wipes the tears you weep
no one cares the amount
that flows endlessly down your cheek
We must take the risk to love
we must dare ourselves to feel
for only then will our lives be filled
and our wounds truly healed

Wounded Bird

The wind flies like a wounded bird
wounded but flying without fear
on its wings, it carries my words
that only you can hear
Through an open window
and softly to your ears
this wind ruffles your blanket
and my sentiment is clear
The wind flies like a wounded bird
but blinded by emotion it is unhurt
for with your essence in its path
you give this bird new birth
With every breath you take
you give this bird new life
with every loving look
you give this bird more strength
the strength to keep on flying
however long the length

Her Eyes

Like a goddess
she looks at me
below the surface
to the depths beneath
She sees my desires
she sees my needs
my being an open book
she can hold and read
With those beautiful eyes
she views my heart
peering at its pages
she knows my every want
Her eyes watch windows
the windows to my soul
of me she has complete understanding
all knowledge of me she holds
Her eyes the marvelous color
of the finest cinnamon ground
Her eyes the exquisite shade
of the earth's deepest brown

Loneliness Like Love

Loneliness holds me like a love
I've known for an eternity of nighttimes
except her touch is cool
like a long-left-vacant leather seat,
and not soft but hard
like rocks under bare feet.

Loneliness holds me like a love
I've known in infinite midnights
except the words she says are sharp
like splinters from tamaracks,
not tough enough to cut
but leaving blue heart bruises eyes must acknowledge

Loneliness holds me like a love
I've known for all seasons
Hugging me every summer,
kissing me each spring,
falling for me in autumn,
but leaving me cold and gray
like winter in Ithaca

Loneliness holds me like a love
I've known for all seasons.

Complete Beauty

By what do they call you
A common name would not suit you
for eyes have not beheld a vessel
that was so completely beautiful
Such absolute purity
complete sincerity throughout
your mind—a fountain of knowledge
leaking brilliance from your mouth
Maybe your name is Nevaeh
heaven—only in reverse
for instead of dwelling in heaven
you reside here on Earth
Forsaking unbroken harmony
to walk amongst man
It would be an honored privilege
if by your side I could stand
Perhaps your name is Luna
basking those who gaze in amazement
a marvel worshipped by the stars
frozen in awe of your marvelous phases

Bathing those below in moonlight
a celestial symbol of hope
if only night were eternal
I would peer forever with my scope
To the end of the Earth I would travel
bear the force of the four winds
if it promised the possibility
to enjoy your presence again

One Wish

If words carried images,
which words would carry you
if pictures flew on the wings of phrases
which phrases would feature you
Only words well and perfect
all phrases honest and true
but it seems not even these things
are worthy to describe you
If I were to wish upon a star
each night of my life
each star would hear the same plea
for I possess only one desire
The heavenly bodies descending
would hear only one request
for there is only one desire
of the heart within this chest
With each setting sun
and every rising of the moon
I would gaze into the heavens
and wish for one more day with you

I Want to Go

I want to go,
where the days are always clear
the horizon is bright, nothing to fear
where all day the sun will shine
there are no shadows, not a cloud in the sky
The sun—a majestic yellow orb
draped in a grand canopy of blue
where the waves break softly
and it's just me and you

I want to go,
where moonlight fills the night sky
As a silver sphere in a blanket of stars
giving me just enough light
to see your face, and the absence of flaws
In this place there are no worries
all cares for a moment   brushed aside
and your sweet voice is the only thing
that breaks the sound of the tide

Against My Destiny

There was nothing I could do
I had lost my source of hope
my life filled with sorrow
doubt gripping my scope
Such hopelessness I felt
when I considered my position
to be lifted from this place
seemed to me needless wishing
But all in a single moment
my outlook was changed
by whom there is only one
for no angels are the same
Like a light at the end of the tunnel
to a troubled soul, you brought peace
bringing a great calmness
that my restless soul was seeking
No matter the distance between
our connection must never cease
for to lose your soothing spirit
would be against my destiny

An Embrace

I sense your presence
and your hair touches my face
I take you into my arms
and cherish the soft embrace
Your warmth pierces through me
your body so close to mine
as I hold your body
thoughts of you hold my mind
Slowly, you begin to let go
and our chests move apart
but as your body drifts away
like a thief, you steal my heart
I look into your eyes
it seems the windows of heaven are open
your lips slowly begin to part
the words of an angel about to be spoken
But I could let no words pass
through those two exquisite lips
for as you stole my heart from me
from you, I stole a kiss

River of Beauty

I wish to speak
of the sweetness
that into you God has sewn
for as the winding Nile
Beauty in you just flows
Through the strands of your hair
then round about your neck
falling off your shoulders
swirling about your chest
trickling down your abdomen
pausing for a moment on your hips
then cascading downward
with a smooth quickness
Flying by your thighs
careening between your knees
a river of beauty
completed at your feet

I wish to speak
of the sweetness
that into you God has sewn
For as the winding Nile
Beauty in you just flows

Five Minutes

What is five minutes?
A collection of rolling moments
tolling on spinning Swiss arms
Or the most amazing path from past to future
that passes seamlessly by
that you wish you could grasp and hold still

What is sixty seconds?
A prolonged portion of existence
spanning the space of a numbered face
or three score of clicking ticks that you can't grab
no matter the effort placed into holding on

What is   that?
That span of time that just slides by
Or a speck of ecstasy that you would place
on permanent pause and repeat continually
but it's gone before you notice

        It depends whether I'm with you.

For times by your side never creep by
But fly on wings much higher than I can reach
Like a song that's done once you get the courage to sing
Or a ball that's caught once you see to swing
Moments with you just go—and I wish I could
slow the flow and fully know the beauty that is you.

So Simple

I think of you at two times
and those times are day and night
because behind my eyes
you are forever in my mind's line of sight
Moments in your presence are a treasured possession
for my mind and heart are under no pressure
Sharing our nears and dears, our doubts and fears
bringing thoughts to the front that once resided in the rear
Through stories of laughter, conflict, and rebuttal
Through casual conversation, we learn from each other
That lack of oppression breeds valued expression
knowledge is heightened and ignorance lessened
true companionship is truly a blessing
and should be valued above all earthly treasures
Forgive this attempt at sounding intellectual
and weaving something so simple into a web of complexity
So forget those phrases prior to these lines
dismiss all the meter, rhythm, and rhyme
all of that gibberish masked within words with many
syllables

remember only this message, I will try and make it simple
I think of you at two times
and those times are day and night

Behind Your Eyes

I sit and wonder what wonders
lie within your mind
as you lie beside me
and closed are your eyes
Of what do you think
of what do you dream
I would like to think
that you dream of me
What does your heart desire
for what do you truly wish
those answers behind your eyelids
I only wish to bear witness
If only I could see
just glance at your fantasies
I would focus for a moment
and commit them all to memory
Then from that wishful realm
those dreams I would remove
and with my hands I would do my
best to mold them into truth

Honestly

Your eyes are a green
the leaves wish they could possess
and the sun cannot match the warmth
of the heart within your chest
Roses envy the redness
that lies within your lips
and true rhythm and blues
wishes for the rhythm in your hips
Your vibrance rivals
that of the first season
for the light of your smile
could change winter into spring
Your eyes looking upward
would cause clouds to flee
for the sun would cast its chasing light
enabling all to see
You must forgive my honesty
but to you I must be truthful
There is nothing in this universe
that could claim to be more beautiful

You Are

I gently take your hand
and look into your eyes
how they do resemble,
the stars in the sky
If I could give you the world,
all of the silver and gold
emeralds, rubies, and diamonds
every single precious stone
all of these riches and more
would never be enough
for the value of your smile
these things could never touch
In your lips you hold
the softest kiss
Everyday without you
is a day of heaven missed
In your presence is eternal bliss
It is true that on earth
an angel does exist
So as I stare into

the ocean of your eyes
I see everything
I ever had in mind
beautiful, generous,
intelligent and kind
patience, tenderness,
blessed peace of mind
I want you to be with me,
forever by my side
my one and only partner
on this journey through life

Proposal

I think of you
and I'm lost in a sea of thoughfulness
feet, knee, chest, neck deep
in an ocean of your memory
Now around, above, beneath,
surrounding me
I.

        Breathe.

Inhaling
your remembrance
Exhaling
your remembrance
removed from reality
consumed by your remembrance

You are beautiful—
There is just no other way to say it
beautiful to me
beautiful to everyone
Those who do not agree

their mind's eyes must be blinded
for even those without sight
can sense your loveliness

I look into your eyes
and I see my future
because for the next five,
ten, fifteen, twenty or more minutes
I could continually glimpse the windows to your soul
in the sole hope to know you better

I hold your hand and I feel an extension of myself
as my half has become whole and my heart
is no longer an empty bowl but now over-
flows with the fullness of you

I kiss, I kiss, I kiss your lips
and I am lifted up, off, and above this earth
until I can no longer sense it beneath me

Will you have me?
not a portion and not a piece
but all of me

Will you grant me consecutive esca-
lating moments of ecstasy
because every day would be a double bless-
ing to wake up and have you next to me
You know you have the best of me
don't expect anything less from me
Here's my hand, you have my heart
let me know when you are ready for the rest of me

I am before you
ring outstretched, perched on one knee
Please allow me the opportu-
nity to try and make you happy

If the answer to this request is *yes*
then like the song says, meet me some-
where only we know—
that nook by the park brook where I read
you poems from my first notebook

that upper deck terrace on the ferry
where I held you after that fight with your parents

the loft in the barn on my granddaddy's farm
that bail of hay where sweetness we made

Meet me somewhere only we know
because there's no place I'd rather go
to escape the furious pace of life's race
and unveil things to brighten this unlightened present
and blaze a path full of promise and poetry

Let's go somewhere only we know
and love will meet us there
and leave us to do what we came to do
and we will do what we came to do
over and over and over
until that creek stops flowing, the sun starts to show
or those cows finally do decide to come home

just let me know if you want to go
somewhere only we know.

No Comparison

I am not well off, well traveled, or well read, I have few possessions and can only offer you true words from this pen.

Mirrors are blessed by your reflection
angels envy your silhouette
and every night as slices of moonlight
pour through the blinds of our bedroom window
I am reminded that I am blessed to lay beside you
Your face sweetens my days
and your smile validates my existence
for when you are happy, I am complete
and when you cry I am torn to pieces

You asleep is a beautiful peace
and when I close my eyes
I reopen them quickly to be sure I am not dreaming
I hold you at night because I don't
want you to disappear
every day is like fantasy and I fear
one day I will wake up and you were never real

Moments with you are pieces of sweet
that my memory eats when the tides
of life rise and my heart is under
the bitter waves of experience
To glimpse the birth of day
as dawn stretches her arms over the horizon
and reflects upon the face of the ocean
I believe the world would agree is beautiful

But as your eyelids open, and your lips part ways—
even the most amazing fade in comparison

Insignificant

Silence
 and I lost my surroundings
 as you passed
 There was only you
 a pearl with no shell
 all else was insignificant
Your face was like the view from a mountaintop
Your hair—like the falls
Your walk—like the wind
your smile—lightning at midnight
your dimples—lagoons of beauty

The bend of your cheek
the ease with which you blink
flashing the hidden brilliance
that lies just beneath
The lush of your lips
the crest of your nose
an essence as such
endless canvas could not hold

No Rembrandt or Picasso
Diego or Kahlo
Rodin or Van Gogh
Rafael or Donatello
No artist could envision
the masterpiece that I see
for standing here is more than man
'tis something heavenly

Essence of Beauty

You are a dream
and when one awakens
 there is left only the longing to dream of you again
You are a flower
that blooms with each rising sun
 and with the light of each ray—we are blessed to
behold your blossom
You are the beautiful colors
the treasures of the third season
 lasting only for days, as the autumn fades to gray
You are a star that passes swiftly overhead
leaving behind a trail of grace
 then disappearing deep into the cosmos behind heaven's gates
You are a blanket
of a season's first fallen snow
that has yet to be tread upon by man, only touched by
the shine of the horizon
You are a crystal river
whose water is untainted

quenching the deepest thirst the instant it is tasted
You are a melody
only those silent can hear
 in the most pure pitch of the sweetest music massag-
ing the drums of the ears

You are a blissful dream, the fullest flower
an autumn day, a soaring star, a freshwater spring
a soothing melody, and if I were to speak
until all breath left—
 I could not speak all that you are to me
You are every kind gift
all things enjoyable
 the sole reason that I am joyful
To my mind
your presence brings such peace
 you are the essence of beauty

Place Your Palm

Place your palm in mine
and walk with me through time
feel our fingers intertwined
as we stand side by side
hold my hand, handle my heart
the warmth from your fingertips
caresses my soul, as light does the dark

Engage my fleeting gaze
our minds' eyes collide
your eyelids as windows, slowly rise
and I behold the beauty inside
Your ivory green irises,
enclosed in a ring of obsidian
penetrate my viewing pupils
and capture my being's vision

Follow your floating feelings
as you fly on the wings of fate
descend upon your destiny
for there, I anxiously wait
In my palm, your palm is placed
and my gaze, by yours has been engaged
Here my heart is at home
and I will never leave this place

A Tender Song

I stand in front of an open window
a soft breeze ruffles my white tee
as the waves break softly, on a sandy beach
and gulls glide gracefully over the sea
But above all these wondrous things
I notice a lady on a faraway dock
softly singing a song
I am caught by her anthem
At first, I cannot hear
but at once the beach goes silent
The sound of her voice is clear
As it made its way through the quiet
I continued to and the world disappeared
Nothing on earth existed,
but her voice and my ears

I Am Going to Miss You

I know that you are leaving,
yes I know that for a fact
but also know that you're not even gone
and I already want you back
You have looked into my eyes
not once, not twice—but a million times
and to think that this gaze is the last
thoughts of emptiness fill my mind
Your words I have looked to for comfort
and for the same you have come to me
we have been there for each other
for calming company
But now these words
must be said over the phone
and feelings shared from miles away
from the pages of my everyday
fate has removed your face
We will be separated

by miles and miles of land
but always understand that in any instant
I will help you if I can
As you travel far from me
I send my best wishes
with a tearful goodbye
rich in hugs and kisses
Some believe that all good things
must sometime come to an end
but in this case it is untrue
because you will always be my friend

Thinking of You

I am thinking of you again
this has to be the millionth time
that your face, your eyes, your smile
have moved across my mind
Visions of you consume my thoughts
I become lost in my imagination
losing all concentration
remembering our last conversation
Behind my eyelids exists an alternate world
filled with your elegant form
I feel a peace come to mind
everything so calm—so warm
Like a child going to its mother
my mind in you feels comfort
Remembering the touch of your hand
places me in a dreamlike trance
If my thoughts were the wind
they would always blow your way
If my thoughts were nomads
in you—they would find a resting place

Assumed Happiness

Sitting with all of his possessions around him
He swims in an ocean of material
Flat-screen plasma televisions
look into masterpieces on the opposite walls
Fine furniture, decoratively arranged
sits in place on the floor
The landscaped lawn of this gated neighborhood
seems like a foundation for happiness

But in his hands, he holds a note
from his wife he barely knows
She's taken his son to her sister's house
whenever he decides to come home
Not his body to come home
but his mind, body, and soul too
because for days, months, years
they all have been at work

Now he holds himself
in a web of indecision
made of two arms
meant to be holding someone else.

Assumed Emptiness

She places her beloved in bed
soon after the ends of sitcoms
and sits in her house coat
wishing she had someone worthy—
worthy enough to remove it

Night's darkness has crept into her
and lost in her imagination
she dreams of being taken
After the twists of evening dramas
and before late-night comedies
her eyelids gain weight
and she drinks from the creek of dreams
Only to awake and begin this again
Wading in this sea of assumed emptiness

She is beautiful, but no one tells her
Lovely, but she never hears it
Something, something important is missing.

Gone Too Soon

With a hand placed to her lips
she spoke softly
in a flurry of wishfulness
wishing to give the meaning
of an inner piece
with minimal confusion

But like a summer thunderstorm
she was here and then gone
but like the rainbows left behind
she left a promising song
playing on the records of my heart

Always an Actress

Part after part
role after role
character after character
she plays everyone
except herself

Scripts dictate her every action
as if her life were parenthesized
The tone of her words
seem inflections of the last director
or perhaps the one before him
or before or before
or perhaps it was the first
but always she is false

Her face made up by Mary Kay
her expressions painted every day
and I am her partner each time we conversate
as if I too am on tape or stage

Who are you…..really?

I'd like to know.

In Due Season

With a quiet contentment
she quietly stains the page
only glancing up
with orbs of blue brilliance
to grasp the inspiration
strewn about her

Richly sparse in her verse
like a wintry wheat field
holding in the life of today
to release it in due season

Few times she has ever
raised her voice
but she will forever
raise her pen

She Is a Year

Her eyes
are like
two spheres
of springtime,
holding the greenness
of an entire
season
in two orbs
that seem
to swirl while
staying
still.
Her skin
says
forever summer
her hair
holds autumn,

but nothing of her is winter.

Like a Tree

She rests in a rocking chair
feet warmed by burning wood
on a Sunday evening
after a dinner of broken buttered biscuits and gravy
smiling—in faith-filled expectancy

Like a teak tree planted
by the waters of the Amazon
she is a constant pillar
bending with the winds of change
but rooted so deep in her upbringing
that breaking is not an option

I admire her strength, stability
and graceful patient growth
one ring at a time

She Knows

She sits ...
on an unelevated
pedestal
before us
Pouring out
knowledge
like a
brick mason
pours concrete
carefully
into a
foundation
Laying a
rock
and a hard place
for our hearts and
minds to stand on
Confident
that with words
we may move the Earth

Imperfect Reflection

In her reflection
she sees vast imperfection
and stares at scars
where others see beauty marks
Her self-confidence
always in question
though others speak differently
upon inspection
Blemishes she says
cover herself
as she desires the features
always of someone else
Her flaws are imagined
for we see a Mona Lisa
but she sees anything
other than a masterpiece

Please open your eyes
gaze down into the pool
and see for the first time
the beauty we have always seen in you

From Something Deeper

She sits in insightful silence
waiting for her turn to speak
smiling politely
and shifting her seat
Sometimes letting it pass
but other times
unleashing sweet speech
slow and sure
like a creek in the woods
not knowing the source
or where it goes
but obvious that it draws from something deep
and leads to something greater

You Are the Reason

May I speak
with the wrinkles in your cheeks
or walk in the paths
of your passing crow's feet
Master motions
of your massaging hands
build half the castles from stone
that you did with sand

To some you are a sister
to one you are a wife
but to me you are the reason
I am what I am in life
I thank you for your teaching
I thank you for your guidance
For you are the reason
I am what I am in life

She Danced

My mouth—
quiet.
As words flew from me like canaries from cages
that yearn to feel real wind beneath their wings.

My pen—
still.
As verse could not convey the grace
with which she moved across the stage

Making amazing with her hands
Forming magnificent with her hips—

She danced.
Radiant and smiling, filling the room with her light
Captivating as she captured, the rhythm
of life—with her movement
Brilliant she was as I watched in awe
I could do nothing but applaud when it was over and
hope to clap hard enough that she would do it all again.

She danced.

And the audience agreed
An encore was in order
And before I could absorb this shine of a shoot-
ing star, this sight of a lightning strike
I bore witness to beauty again.

She danced. She danced. She danced.

Every move was memorable. Every
gesture was a blessing
and I smile every time I remember the
moment when I think her eyes met mine.

She danced.

Not Quite

I thought her hand could live in mine but then it decided to move away—as if the flower I had found to be a lily was only a day-living morning glory and dusk had come with no promise of another sun.

She decided that to bloom again wasn't worth the risk and I was left trying to salvage the image of her petals all together, while trying to understand why she would let herself wilt.

We met and I found myself falling for her movement, lost in her loveliness and looking back at delightful every time she looked at me.

Her purity challenged my faithfulness to grow and with each passing moment in me grew hope that she would choose me too.

But as cold winds of change began to blow and uncertain skies began to show, her blossom decided to close to protect the preciousness inside.

You and Me

1

I love the way your hair lays in your face but your hand
does not whisk it away because it's too busy sewing
poem patches on a blank page.

2

Your face takes the words from my throat and
hushes me to a muted silence and you tell me
that you know I don't know what to say. I've
fallen for you like oak leaves in autumn time
that just don't want to fight anymore…

3

Lay your head on my chest and feel what you're
responsible for.

4

You or performance. Performance. Me or work. Work.
Together or apart. Apart.

5

Our lives are driving in different directions and we are both too busy watching the road to notice we've taken different exits.

6

Fate placed you in my path and time erased you from the pages of my every day.

7

me.   you.

Dripping Diamond

My window is open
I stand to look out
and I see the clouds rolling in
a storm approaching from the south
My gaze remains upward
dark clouds will soon hide the sun
a mother calls to her children
and they beg to continue their fun
My eyes drift downward
and they descend upon a couple
raindrops begin to fall
but they exhibit no rebuttal
They only laugh and smile
clasping each other's hands
and as the rain falls faster
they come to a stop and stand
Though the weather is contrary
and they are drenched in raindrops
he falls to a knee
and removes a moist velvet box

Because I am above
I am unable to hear his words
I can only imagine
his amazing arrangement of nouns and verbs
Perhaps he told
of the pleasant sound of her voice
or that when she speaks
silent goes all noise
Maybe the way she quivered slightly
when that first kiss was received
the softness of her skin
or that spot on the back of her knee
Perhaps he told her of all things
that set her apart
and of that special moment
when she captured his wandering heart
No doubt his words were honest and sweet
for she accepted the dripping diamond
as he knelt at her feet

In The Paper

I pick up the local paper
just to catch up on the news
the headlines flash a pending war
but not even that can hold my view
For in the bottom right corner
at the lowest point of my glance
I see the love of my life
engaged in her first wedded dance
She is held in the same arms
that inflicted so much pain
staring into the same eyes
that showed so much rage
How could the softest rose
of such passion and promise
reject a garden of tenderness
for a barren field of drama
How could she forsake a home
of understanding and hope
carelessly dashing them away
like trash through an open window

I once loved that lady
with my entire being
a beautiful future with her and I
was the vision I was seeing
But I too was tossed out
cast away for reasons unknown
Hurled into a world of doubt
caught in an emotional cyclone
To think that my love was unwanted
that my love was not good enough
sent me down an abyss of self confidence
a real life sea of hopelessness
Now though my heart was bruised
my feelings did not disappear
For I fell back into the web
at the first sight of her dropping tears
Apparently she had left me
for a man that loved by day
but in the night that same man
opens a bottle and drifts away
Transforming into an abusive brute
rendering her blind, deaf, and mute
She only sees the black of her eyes
only hears yelling and broken glass

who could she tell, for who would believe her
over a man of supposed stature and class
So I nursed the wounds
with kind words that soothed
sweeping away the worries
like a mother's kitchen broom
But as soon as the eyes were open
and the bruises were gone from her limbs
she left the comfort of my arms
and went quickly back to him
Again I was used for my sensitivity
manipulated like Einstein's formula
for the theory of relativity
Abandoned once again
like a used coloring activity
So as I stare down at this society page
and see the smile on her face
I hope a smile it stays
Though I was hurt and my heart broken
My love will never fade away

As I ... the Lonely Go

Is there a place for the dejected
here on earth, beneath the heavens
a place for those who pretend not to be effected
by the recurring rejection and lack of affection
A place for the emotionally burdened
a home for the hearts of nice guys
who are tired of hurting
A bed for those, so tired of being unloved
a dwelling place for wandering spirits,
surely there is one
For as I stand in the droves at the corner store
and view a man purchase a single rose
It's February 14th and I mutter to myself
where do I, the lonely go

As the years go by and the years come and go
and I have yet to bring a lady to my mother's home
I watch my friends marry, and their children grow
I wonder, where do I—the lonely go
As I stroll down the streets on Christmas Eve

and a couple makes tracks in the fallen snow
They walk happily hand in hand—
oblivious to the cold
and I shivering wonder—where do I, the lonely go
There is no place for me, in this abyss
this swirling whirlpool of unhappiness
I have waited for love and that love has never come
I search for friends, and I can find not one

Now I stand atop a building,
and I step out onto the edge
I lean my head back, and let my hands let go
as the wind rushes past,
and the ground doth approach
I wonder just where, just where the lonely go

Only In My Dreams

Only in my dreams
have I ever had the chance
to hold you in my arms
or even touch your hand
Only in my imagination
only in my restful mind
had such bliss ever existed
had I ever experienced a moment so fine
Your hair, soft as a tranquil wind
the sweet smell of your fragrant skin
your loving eyes looking back at me
the color of a deep tropical sea
but all of this has only been a dream
never has this ever been a reality
But as I open my eyes tonight
your head lays softly on my chest
and I can smell your fragrance
every time I take a breath
In that instant, happiness flowed
from the edge of my being

to the very depths of my soul
I feel that if God looked down
and told me to let you go
I would pull you even closer
look above and tell him, "No."
For this night my heart is complete
within my soul—absolute peace
and as you lay sound asleep,
I realize true has come my deepest dream

Fresh Meadows

I get on the F-train at 50th Street
headed to Fresh Meadows, Queens—
say, "Excuse me," and take my subway seat
My tired eyes once closed, steal a glance next to me
viewing beauty as such my eyes had never seen

I did not speak,
but oh how I wanted to speak
words that would sow seeds
and spring more speech between I and she

All it would take was hello or hi
before the next stop meant a permanent goodbye

I feel like I'm in the Wizard of Oz
wanting the bravery of Richard the Lionhearted
but I have no quest, no noble crusade
I have only one moment, one day, one train
and I have only one question—
what is her name?

I open my mouth and silence falls out
the subway doors open, she stands and steps out

Oh, she forgot her cell phone
what to do now—this

Her cell in one hand, my heart in the other
I throw open the closing doors and try not to stutter

"Miss, Miss, you forgot this,"
she turns, eyes wide and inquiring
she looks down in her purse
and then up and smiling
"I'm so glad you found it."

"Just glad that I could help,"
bursts out before anything else
An awkward silence ensues
and I'm not sure of what to do
The F-train just left
and I guess I should wait for another one
it would be awfully nice to wait with someone
I must have been thinking out loud
because she asked where I was from

Time flashes by and here another F-train is
so I asked if I could call her
on the very phone that I had given

She replies with a slip of paper
and says tomorrow she's free for dinner
Goodbye was said and she walked away
and again I boarded that same F-train.
I said, "Excuse me," and took my seat
headed with a smile to Fresh Meadows, Queens.

Dinner for Two

I chose the Rainbow Room because the view was almost as breathtaking as her face and I let her order whatever she wanted because it's the closest I get to giving her the world. This is just nice.

There were other couples having dinner, a live orchestra, and a child that wanted everyone to know he didn't belong there but I just could not notice them when she looked at me. With the wine and food just taken by the waiter and dessert on the way she met my gaze and gave me a glimpse of those dimples.

"You're so different," she said and then asked, "why?"

I replied without thinking, "It's because I'm a Christian," and the silence that ensued was deafening.

Quietness was all I heard as her face changed beats after the words left my lips and plucked her eardrums. She just sat there—contemplating every preconceived notion of the Christianity that she knew and didn't agree with. Attempting to mend the damage done by Catholic Priests in the media, overzealous evangelicals, and the countless seasons of the 700 *Club* I looked at her and said, "but I'm not like them" and her eyes said she didn't believe me.

I told her how I spoke to a congregation in Virginia Beach the week before and a young boy sat down front with the top of his jeans meeting the backs of his thighs. My Mom looked to me before I took the podium and whispered, "they *think* they're alright."

She laughed and asked, "So what did you say to them?"

"That four walls and a steeple don't change the way you are. Knowing and quoting Bible verses don't alter your daily life. It's only when you live those scriptures that your life begins to take on a new meaning and then people will start to ask you . . . why are you so different?"

She smiled.

With the tiramisu just removed, I put on my jacket and helped her with hers. We stepped into the elevator and both of us watched the numbers descend to the illuminated 1 and I wondered what thoughts wandered through her mind. I hailed the taxi and we both got in. I put my arm around her and she leaned in close. We talked about the different paths our lives had taken but we were so happy to be in this place at this time.

"I think I'm gonna take that job at the Bailey House. You know the AIDS Shelter I told you about?" I asked.

"Yes, I remember," she said not excited. "I got an offer from Goldman this morning."

"Congratulations," I quickly replied. "You gonna take it?"

She sat up for a moment, "Absolutely, the bonus potential is one hundred fifty percent. I'd be crazy not to accept it."

She rested her head back on my chest and I couldn't help but reflect on those two paths.

"Do you think that I shouldn't..." I began but the cab reached its destination before I could finish. I almost wished he would just drive around the block because this ride was definitely worth the fare. I walked her to her door and she kissed me like it was the last time, said "goodnight" and with the turn of a key she disappeared behind her oak door.

I turned and waved the cabby on, I could take the subway back to Hamilton Heights. I looked up at the streetlights hoping to see stars and remembered what my granddaddy used to say, "Two people cannot walk together unless they agree." I looked at the closed door and wondered if she would pray before she went to bed, probably not; but I knew that I would.

Do You Know
What It's Like

"But a time is coming, and has come, when you will be scattered, each to his own home. You will leave me all alone. Yet I am not alone, for my Father is with me.

John 16:32 (NIV)

Expecting

February 28, 1986, Ana Sophia Valdez was born, but she wasn't supposed to be. The doctors said things like, "your platelet count is too low" and "your body can't handle a full term pregnancy"; but all I could think that her name was going to be named after mi bis-abuelita–ella era una grande mujer...

Blue was going to be the color of her nursery; not baby blue, but the kind of blue that's almost green como la bahia del pirata. It's so beautiful there. Mi hermana Patricia told me that I had enough diapers for three babies not just the one on the way and that I said enough prayers for the next generation, so I should be covered in the delivery room. eight months and three days passed, and laying on the hospital bed the need of prayers was obvious but the need of diapers was put into question.

Mi chiquita-linda had made it this far and my body wouldn't let her out. I prayed for two more centimeters but did not have two more centimeters to give and then I heard it. "Is she a hemophiliac?"

"Claro que no," I said.

"Can I get a platelet count," said Dr. Gonzalez to the attendant.

"Nine thousand parts per million" she replied, "she should be around 250,000."

"Sofia, we're going to have to do an emergency C-section," the nurse said to me in an assertive tone. "Mr. Valdez, I'm going to have to ask you to leave." He had never left me. "Mrs. Valdez, this is going to pinch a bit."

I awoke to hear two sets of beeps—the beeping of my own EKG machine, but also of mi hija. Smiles were all around me as mi familia looked down at our little Ana. For two days, I watched her listening to the beeps. March 3, a Wednesday, the nurse asked if I wanted to hold her. With tears I said yes. "Mi angelita."

Twenty years later Ana is gone and su padre tambien. College called my chiquita-linda far away and differences pushed mi corozon to another place. I am in a new house with a new man and his four children; and for the second time—I am pregnant. With a plus sign in the indicator I smiled a smile only a mother can—a smile of promise, of life. Nothing in this new place was mine and looking at Jeff, nothing in this new house was ours. This was a chance, this was our chance ...

Jeffrey Kent Wright was supposed to be born on April 10, but he wasn't. The doctors said things like, "Your platelet count is too low" and "your body can't handle a full term pregnancy"; but it was followed by "this hospital has the best obstetricians in the country and you and your baby are going to be just fine." With a smile I thought to myself his name was going to be Jeffrey Kent Wright, after his father—Jeff would really like that.

Blue was going to be the color of his nursery; baby blue, just like the flag I saw when I got off of the train at Ana's college.

Eight weeks in I awoke, saying "Aye, aye dios." Stomach hurting, stomach hurting bad. Jeff walked me to the bathroom and I saw the spots of blood. He called 9-1-1.

At the hospital I lay again on the table, stomach small and heaving.

"Can I get a platelet count?" the Doctor Johnson said.

"Ten thousand parts-per-million," replies the attendant, "should be around 250,000."

I kept bleeding—so open when I wanted to be

closed, my mind holding on when my body was slowly letting go. "¿Pasa algo? Diganme por favor!" I screamed, bleeding. I bled until it was over and they carried him out in a bucket.

I couldn't sleep the first night because I heard no beeping. Knees up to my chest, curled into myself, I only thought of what could have been. If I closed my eyes I could see him, brown hair and dark eyes and a nose like his grandfather's—mi hijo.

The sun rose and soon it was time for me to go. Stomach still paining, I sat in a chair and waited to be wheeled out. "Are you ready to go," said Jeff. "Si," I nodded. That night by my bedside I saw him–tall with brown eyes and dark hair y un nariz como su abuelo. Softly he said, "Mamita, it's alright. No te preocupas, no llores. Estoy muy bien. Buenas noches Mamita, buenas noches."

Blown Away

Jim spins the barrel of a .45 and tries to find a reason not to end his life. He can't—his life is trash and he pulled the trigger five times trying to throw himself away. Maybe there's a reason the single bullet is in the sixth barrel and his brain isn't plastered on the cracked paper behind him.

"Death is so much easier than dealing with the world around you, isn't it?"

There is no one there so he answers.

"Yes."

There was a click and not a bang but he should not be here anymore—exactly, there should be no more him at all. Disbelief, discontent, disappointment lies on his face. He should be descending towards that engulfing darkness or lifting towards that consuming light that Christians talk about, but instead he's still here. Maybe his dad was right when he said that Jim could never finish anything he started. Dad was never there anyway so what difference did it make what he said. Mom did a job of standing in for him—her shadow did anyway.

"I'm just like this gun," he says, "worthless." He chucks it through the air of the living room. It strikes the front door and a single shell comes flying back in the direction it was thrown. He ducks with the sound and the bullet lodges itself in the wallspace where his head used to be.

"D-mn it," he says, standing up, "F-cking sh-t," kicking over the thrift store coffee table, spilling the contents of a dead potted plant onto the uncovered hardwood.

"What do I do now?"

Seconds, minutes, passing and still Jim just stands. Finally his feet head to the kitchen, Honey Nut Cheerios crash into a glass bowl and milk fills up its circular crawlspaces. He starts to eat. The sound of crunching pierces the silence, strikes the walls and reverberate in the empty air. Crunch, crunch, crunch. The spoons pings the unfilled bowl and Jim sits in quietness, alone. Again. Always alone.

A faint flop is heard as his mail comes sliding through the crack in the door. Rising from the chair, he walks over to the mat where no one but him has ever wiped their feet, gathers the paper, takes them to the trash and drops them in. Then he starts to pace back to the chair from where he came. Looking back into the bowl, he finds a lone cheerio. Lifting it to his lips he pours the remaining contents into his mouth. Meanwhile a knock shatters the silence, startling him so much that the bowl slips from his grasp and not reaching out fast enough it strikes the floor and spreads itself over the linoleum. After silent moments pass Jim, sitting in a pit of himself and broken glass, sees strange fingers slide a package notice into the mail slot.

Jim watches the pink slip float down and goes on to read it trying to avoid cutting his sockless feet. The slip reads: Greenville Penitentiary, 1000 Prison Road, Emporia, Virginia 23868 and the box for "left on front porch" is checked. Opening the door, picking up the package, and quickly slamming it shut, Jim stalks over to the kitchen table and places the box on the placemat. Looking down at his now bleeding foot, he removes a piece of glass and uses it to cut the thick tape. Once open, Jim cries. Tears pour onto the two photographs, seep into the three pairs of thick black socks, leak into the pile of notebook paper and soak the handwritten letter lying on top of it all. From James Jeremiah Johnson, Sr.—born January 16, 1956, and executed January 16, 2006.

Dear Son,

I love you. No matter what the family said, I love you. I don't know if you got the packages I sent you on your birthday or the letters I wrote every week. You never wrote back but I never stopped writing. I don't know where you are or what you're doing but I want you to know I think about you everyday. Me and your mom did some bad things as you're probably well aware but I couldn't bear the thought of both of us in here and you out there all alone so I took the weight of the consequences, myself. We fought before she left the visiting room the last day I saw her about that, and I don't think she ever forgave me for going to prison, but I hope that you can. I hope you went to school and got good grades and maybe even got into college. I wonder sometimes if you were a doctor or a lawyer...but if you're a car mechanic or in the army, that's great too. I'd just be happy to know that you were doing okay. I found God while I was in here, son, or better yet He found me and I could spend all of this letter telling you about what's happened the last twenty years or I could pray that you make it to heaven and tell you in person when we get there. My crimes aren't important; you can read about them in the paper or on the news, but my forgiveness won't be on the front pages of anything. Know that I got a second chance, not because my circumstances changed, but because God changed me in my circumstance. I wasn't in prison for twenty years, I had been in prison since I left my mother's womb and only sitting in a cell was I finally set free. You don't need a cell to be in prison son, but you need God to find freedom. It's about that time now and they'll be taking me away soon so live the life that I should have, love the woman that you are supposed to, and raise the son I wish I had.

—J. J. Johnson, #49736
January 13, 2006

Jim reads the letter again and again, each sentence resonating in the confines of his mind as he tried to wrap his mind around his father—trying to hug a letter so hard that the man who wrote them feels his embrace.

Don't Leave Me

Don't leave me here
because I don't think
I'm going to make it
Don't leave me here
because I don't think
my heart could take it
Just stay here with me
as long as you can
whisper sweet words
softly hold my hand
Don't leave me here
because I won't make it through
Just stay here with me
because my time is coming soon
Tell me that you love me
tell me that you care
promise me that when I close my eyes
you will still be there
Don't leave me here
because it is cold in this room

and these blankets do not warm me
the same way your arms do
There is no comfort
in the television screen
famous strangers do not compare
to your calming company
Don't leave me here
in the dark, the silence, the alone
Stay here, please just stay
until it is time to go home
my body is so tired
so ails my spirit
speak a sweet word
my heart longs to hear it
I feel exhausted
my soul ready to rest
as a tired runner slows
so does the heart within my chest
…
You did not leave me
but now I must leave you
and when I open my eyes again
I only hope to see you

Ain't No Need

I coulda swore Fairview Baptist Church had one hundred folks in the choir and a thousand in the congregation that Sunday—or better it sho' sounded like it. The pews was full and the deacons had to run and get extra folding chairs to put in the back and even in the aisles cuz folks all squeezin' in tryna' hear that Reverend Baker's homecoming message; at least that's what I figures people was there for. It may have been Miss Betty's potato salad, Wilson Brothers' fried chicken or my Momma's strawberry dumplings that was coming up right after service, but either way, it ain't matter cuz people was there and people was praising the Lord.

I got up 'bout midway through the message to meet the folks from Wilson's barbecue and get everything ready for the repass. Old ladies got to get their plates for husbands that didn't show up and kids needed extra napkins for all that grease. Things was goin' along right smooth. All the food was in place and us ladies was just waiting on the people to start coming up the ramp into the fellowship hall. We could all hear Pastor on the loudspeaker,

"Cuz Lord knows when my work is done down here. I want my Savior to look down at me and say well done, thou good and thou faithful service. Can I get a witness? I said, can I get a witness up in here? Is there any body here that loves my Jesus? I said anyone who know that trouble don't last always. Weeping may endure for a night, but joy—I said joy—sweet joy sho' does come in morning. Amen. Amen. Amen."

"Amen" echoed the congregation and I heard the customary silence that follows after a rousing message as Reverend opened up the altar for prayer. "Time to get your gloves on," said Mary and we all did so taking our places behind the different dishes. All I could think was that it was a wonder all of us won't diabetics. A lifetime's worth of hog and cane on that table in one meal, Lord have mercy, I thought to myself.

Just then sister Rose came hustling through the door with a pot of cabbage. "I's hoping I wasn't gon' be late. Had to get this recipe just right." The flower-patterned pot plopped down beside the rest of the side dishes with her pot holders stuck down in the handles. "I sure do hope they like it," she said and before any of us could greet or reply she was back out the back door heels clicking down the steps.

Next thing I knew I was looking at an empty chicken pan and some mighty happy people sittin' round breaking some bread. Deacons loosening belts, children cutting up, and grandma's tryna see which hat was better. 'Twas a sight to see. While I was looking 'round, just takin' it all in I heard pastor say something.

"I ain't eating it," he said to Miss Betty in a calm voice at the end of the server's table.

"What's wrong with it, Pastor," she replied.

"Don't you trouble yourself about it, just know I ain't eating it and nobody else is either," he said in a more serious tone.

We all just nodded and I moved to pick up the pot of cabbage that had no business being there according to pastor. Taking a big serving spoon I walked on over to the trash and started scoopin' it out. I'da thought nuttin' of it until I got to the bottom of the pot. Crossed in the bottom were a knife and fork. My grandmamma used to tell me about women out here in these woods working with roots and things. I ain't never pay her no mind, but a cross in the bottom of a pot never meant no good to nobody. I looked up from the pot and Reverend Baker's eyes met mines from across the room. He nodded and I nodded and I dropped the pot in the trash along with the cabbage.

With a pitcher in hand I walked across the room to fill the Pastor's glass with sweet tea. I leaned down and said, "now just ain't no need for all that now is it." He took up his glass and replied, "no mam, ain't no need at all."

Proud

Spring semester of my freshman year at Park View High School I walk onto a soccer field with bare-hands and basketball shorts to stand in front of an eight-feet-tall twenty-four-feet wide goal. Coach Fox tosses me gloves and asks, "Are you ready?" I nod my head and position myself in what I assume to be the center and stare at the line of forwards in front of me. "Shoot!" he yells, and the balls begin to fly.

One by one they came, low and to my left side, high and to my right, straight into my chest, over the goal, off my knee, diving to my left the shot just wide—over and over the balls come. Sweat pours down my face, my shirt comes off. The balls continue to come but none continue into the net. The pop of a soccer ball being kicked had to be followed by the thump of it striking my fists—it was like music.

Two weeks later, in the Spring Sports Edition of the South Hill Enterprise in big bold

letters, I read "Park View to Showcase Freshman Goalie."

"Hey Walton, this true?" Kendall says holding the paper up with barbecue dripping from

his fingers. He had been in the deli again.

I take it from his sticky fingers and begin to read the article below the photograph.

"Walton's reflexes are nothing like I've ever seen. It's been two weeks and he's blocking

shots some pros can't get to. I'm proud of him," said the coach.

Proud.

The word chained my eyes to it and would not let go. Proud. A man, proud of me.

"Ah, that's cool Kendall, I'm doing my best," I say still thinking, proud, I've never

heard that before. "I'm gonna take a quick break, cool?"

"That's fine Walton, no problem."

I walk to the bathroom and look into the mirror and my reflection blurs. Proud. Proud. I

didn't know what to do with that so I cried.

I loved being in front of the goal because for the split second after the ball left that shooter's foot, the only obstacle was time and space. Was there time enough for my body to close the space between my hands and the ball and keep the opponent's goal empty. For those few moments, I was not a broken child. I did not live in a house where my father didn't know what grade I was in. I did not have to worry that no one would be waiting for me after the last whistle. I knew that if I stopped that shot, I would be a hero, the crowd would become my family and somebody would roll down their passenger side window to care how I got home that night and I would tell them to leave hoping that my dad would come around the bend and tell me that he was proud.

Firing At Hatred

I awoke to the sound of yelling; the words were inaudible and I struggled to hear. Despite my great efforts, I could make no sense of the chaos that surrounds me. To the left, I see a digital clock, which reads 3:16. My vision then goes to the right of me, where I gaze at the shriveled pillow and wrinkled sheets that once held my wife's form. "Sandy, Sandy," I whisper. No answer. "Sandy, Sandy," I shout in urgency. Then in a blink of silence I hear a soft, "I'm here," as she replies from an unlit bathroom somewhere across the darkness. I sprint to her side and on my way out of habit flick the light switch. "Turn them off," she yells, and as quickly as light filled the room it was plunged back into darkness. Again she fell silent, her knees pulled up to her chin and tears rushing down her pale cheeks. "What's wrong? Just tell me what's wrong," I said to her trying to be of some comfort to a pain I knew not. Her lips quivered but no sound was allowed to pass through them, she only continued to weep unable to speak a word. In response she slowly raised a shivering forefinger to the window across the room. Suddenly, through the very pane of glass on which my eyes were fixed, came a flying brick that shattered the glass into thousands of pieces. "Daddy, Daddy," my son screamed, clutching pants of my pajamas.

Though terribly confused, my mind must stay focused; amid this turmoil I must stay calm. "Sandy, hold him," I say in a calm but commanding voice and make my way gingerly towards the curtains, dodging furniture, and shards of glass. My hand moves toward the curtains, the only shield between me and our front yard and I began to peel back the linen. It was then I beheld it. It birthed a million emotions in a matter of moments. My limbs were struck motionless as my mind struggled to process the events that were taking place. In my yard, where my son and I play catch, in my yard where my wife loves to plant her favorite flowers, in my yard where I plan to spend the most important portions of my life, in my yard, only then feet high but seemingly a tower of flaming hatred stood a blazing cross. The moonlight reflected the flames and cast shadows upon the hooded cowards as they paraded around the figure chanting horrific psalms of ignorance. Every fiber of my being was sent into an uncontrollable rage. With every billow of smoke that rose, so did my feelings of disgust—with every crackling splinter that disintegrated into ash and burned with the fire of hate and discrimination, so smoldered the feelings of resentment in my heart—with every slur emitted from their vocal cords, so responded the cries of two hundred million degraded slaves from my soul. These feelings overwhelmed me and my body reacted to this cyclone of emotions in a puzzled stillness, a hesitant uncertainty that can only be triggered by absolute fear.

"Get out, nigger!" I heard as another brick was hurled toward the shattered crevice where I stood. Frozen in fear, my body did not move, though the hardened clay was visibly headed towards me. It struck me in the chest with the force of infinite cracking whips, a thousand miles of chain, and one ton of confusion. It struck the very core of my being with such an impact that I collapsed upon the floor to wallow in the perceived helplessness to which I had been reduced. I rolled in a tearful, anger-filled agony which words are not worthy of describing. Then, I heard them cheer.

They cheered. They cheered as if they were a group of children at a carnival game and my house was just a booth where you could amuse yourself for fifty cents.

"I got him," one of them yelled in triumph as if I were

just some duck in a row positioned for his entertainment. They exuded happiness in my agony, took pleasure in this demeaning disgrace. Why! I cry out on the inside. Why! Why! Why! My soul screams a thousand times over in a volume so tremendous that it was silent. Then.... bang! I heard its path as it whizzed from the windowsill to the ceiling, then lodged itself in the wall. I heard them as they bombarded my living room, punctured my furniture, pierced my portraits, and desecrated possessions most precious to my family and me. "Daddy, Daddy!" shouted my son. "John, John," shouted my wife. I clutch my family in my arms and struggled to loosen the grip of fear regain some grasp of reality. "John, just make them stop. Please make them stop," said Sandy in a tearful whisper, her head buried in my chest.

My son spoke in an incomprehensible language of shrieks and screams soiling my t-shirt with his tears. I covered the sides of his head trying to keep the frightening sounds from reaching his ears. "Please make them go away," Sandy continued repeating, her requests growing more and more frantic. All of this, as the crowd grows louder and louder and stones pelt my house as a million hens peck at a single grain of seed. "We don't want you here, nigger!" echoes the crowd. My wife, my son, the crowd—my wife, my son, the crowd—these things overtake me. I must make it stop, I must; I can no longer bear these sounds. A great man once said you must fight violence with non-violence; but how can you be still when you stare into the flooding pupils of your wife and son. I must end this. Please, God, make them stop! My fear transformed into anger, and began fueling the urge to protect. Though my thoughts were reduced to shambles and of my actions I was unsure, I scrambled to my knees and then to my feet. I walked somewhat crouched in fear of being struck by another brick or this instance a bullet. A large bruise had formed on my sternum and I clutched my chest as I made my way to the bed. Within the darkness, I felt blindly for my weapon and soon held the long steel shaft between my thumb and forefinger. With no great difficulty, my hand removed the rifle and loaded the barrel to its full capacity. Again I made my way through the darkness to the space from which I had come; as before I moved the curtains back and again beholding the horror below. Again I heard the racial slurs and again terror compelled my spirit to act. I slowly raised the rifle and brought it to rest in position on my collarbone. In a swift motion, I released the safety, cocked the barrel and unleashed my raging retaliation in the form of 2 ½ shells. Bang! I squeezed the trigger and those cries of triumph quickly shifted to confusion. Bang! Bang! Bang! I aimed and began squeezing the trigger again and again until the magazine was exhausted and I heard the unfamiliar click of an empty cartridge clip.

And still I heard this click, click, click, as I continued moving my right forefinger back and forth and forth and back. I was no longer firing at the assailants outside my residence, but at the hatred held within them. I was firing at the epidemic of prejudice that threatened my existence. Then there was silence, an eerie silence that was only occasionally interrupted by the crackling fibers of the enflamed cross.

Innocence Executed

For eight long years I have sat upon death row and finally the day has come that my curtain is going to close. For 243 months, I have been locked inside this cell and for 2920 days, 23 hours, 52 minutes, and 33 now 34 seconds—my life has been nothing short of hell. The moment draws near when I will take my last walk—— and with the victim's family I will have my very last talk. As I finish the last bite of this, my last meal, the concept of death I begin to grasp. To a wooden chair my body will be strapped, and a metal cap put upon my head— electricity will be run throughout my entire body until at last, I am dead. Ten pairs of eyes will stare, gape and gawk, quite possibly enjoying the sight of my life being lost. I remember staring into those same eyes, those same frowning faces. The prosecutor shouting insults, back and forth as he paces. In my own defense I testified, "I wasn't there. I don't even own a gun, so how could I have pointed it and shot someone?"

Upon the truth I swore and all of the words I said were true but all at once the lawyer turned and said,

"Why should they believe you?" In closing arguments, they called me dirty, rotten, and filthy and when the foreman was asked to rise, he handed down a verdict of guilty. All at once I rose to my feet and at the top of my lungs, I began to scream: "I don't belong in prison—get your hands off of me!" I fought as they put cuffs on my hands, and chains on my feet; but it didn't matter what I did—to prison they carried me. Later that month I received my sentence, the words pierce my heart to this day. The foreman again was asked to rise—and before he sat, I was condemned to die.

I haven't seen the stars in eight years, if you could count the drops in the oceans—only then could you begin to count my tears. I am all but forgotten, my family no longer visits me. All I have left are thoughts and memories. My father, how he used to drive the tractor across our farm. My two brothers and I, how we used to play touch football in the backyard. My mother used to cook breakfast on Sunday morning as she sang "Amazing Grace," the love of God, shown off her face. As she kneaded the biscuits, it would go something like this, "Amazing Grace, how sweet the sound that saved a wretch like me. I once was lost, but now I'm found; I was blind, but now I see." I miss you momma. My wife, she had the smile of an angel. I swear you could see wings, if you gazed from just the right angle. The birth of my daughter, she was so small within my arms. I remember the first time she called me Daddy, it filled a void within my heart.

But my third year here, my momma passed away. I missed her funeral, the month of January, that fourth Monday. My wife remarried and my daughter should be thirteen—I am forgotten, no more visiting Daddy. The last bite settles in my stomach and the warden instructs me to rise. I have resolved in my mind that I am going to die. I walk the last one hundred feet, one foot in front of the other—left then right, left then right. The chains clank across the floor, I squint my eyes in the light. I try to turn my wrists but I meet pain—the shackles so tight. I walk into the room, with my head held high. I enter into the witnesses' midst wearing not a frown nor a smile. The executioner asked for my last words and I look each victim in the eyes.

"The state killed me years ago, gave me a number—I no longer had a name. Inmate number 49536, I was not a person anymore; I was a convict. I used to be a man until I came here, now I'm part of an unwanted clan, clasped in chains and wearing orange suits. This was not the way it was supposed to be! Just as your loved one's life was stolen, the state, the judge, the jury—each and every one of you; stole my life from me. I have been raped and beaten, ridiculed, and scorned. I have looked up to God and cursed the day I was born. None of you, have had to say goodbye to your daughter through bullet-proof glass—none of you could look into a file cabinet and see which day on this earth would be your last. My spirit is broken and my heart forever dismayed. My body stands before you, but my mind has passed away." The shackles were secure and the metal cap put into place, as drops from the sponge flowed down my troubled face. "Please Lord, take me quick! I am not worthy of this punishment. You are the only one who can read my heart and you know that I am innocent." I looked over to the wall and the executioner began to reach for the lever. So before the electricity flowed through my veins, once again I look up to heaven. "The Lord is my Shepherd, I shall not want. He maketh me to lie down in green pastures, He leadeth me beside still waters. He restoreth my soul.

He leadeth me on the path of righteousness for his namesake. Yea, though I walk through the valley of the shadow of death … "

Café 212

Holding Twix and Snickers, Twizzlers and licorice, the lighted machine hums a song saying softly food, with its entrails covered by glass-like plastic and its secrets on display and for sale for less than a dollar.

A young girl with a Washington, no taller than five hands, places her right hand on its face and presses hers against it, lets her breath fog it for a moment as her sweet tooth must choose what sweet food she will eat—M&Ms.

So reaching on tip-toes she offers her George for a treat and at first it looks like her fingers won't reach but then the dollar is eaten and nothing happens.

One, then two, then three seconds pass, an eternity of moments and she wonders exactly what's happening; on brink of thinking her George has been stolen, down falls her treat and up she jumps for joy throwing her hand inside to collect her candy.

Retrieving her treat, she says thank you and curtsies in front of the machine, clutches her candy and disappears into the crowd of toddlers and strollers looking for a mom to ask simply, "Will you open this for me?"

Cracked Pecans

July 22, 2003, an empty condom case was code for *he's cheating on your mom* and I chose to try and end my dad's life with a twelve gauge and one full casing. That's where God came in.

My Mom entered the family room, mumbling the Lord's Prayer and I put the barrel to floor. Tears flooded my face and she tried to wipe them away. She looked at me, her face said, *I forgive him.* She hugged me, her arms said, *I forgive you.*

I spent days in high school hoping he wouldn't be home when I came back and spent nights disappointed when he was. And that disappointment didn't disappear when I came home from college the first year ... the second year ... the third year ... that's where God came in.

It's January 7, 2007, and I sit on a couch my father bought on credit, typing on a laptop that I bought for myself and ask my dad, shirtless and shoveling nuts into his mouth if he thought that this was the life that God meant for us?

With a hand full of cracked pecans and peanut shells, his mouth now empty of nuts, he looks at me and says *I guess not.*

He walks away.

I can barely feel the middle finger on my left hand or the pointer finger on my right and when they touch I see the connection but I don't feel it. That's where God comes in.

Whole House, Broken Home

June 5, 1987, I heard a vehicle clambering down Jackson Road and I was anxious to see who would be living in me. Six true individuals emerged. Momma with her hair fried and laid to the side and James Sr. with a freshly picked afro struggled to keep control of three kids that had been buckled up for three hours and were now on the loose. James Jr., J.J. for short, was the oldest, a lanky fifteen, with a brain quicker than a cat of nine tails. He had gone to the best public schools in the country in Fairfax County and his curious eyes and the inquisitive mind behind them never let you forget it. Jeff and Nathaniel were next, two and one, respectively, with only a year and four months between them. Jeff held fast to people and pant legs trying to navigate the terrain. Nathaniel, barely a year old lay in his mother's arms, always close to her heart, or maybe just hoping for another meal. This was the portrait of a family brought back to humble beginnings from the suburbs of Washington, DC, to rest on land that was in Momma's family the last 150 years. It looked like a fairy tale, a husband, a wife, and their little spitting images. Things were never much like that first glimpse I got when they popped out of that station wagon.

A thirty-year-old, J.J. ascended from my basement with a contraceptive in hand and called out for Jeff. Jeff was fifteen years old now and I was praying it could be his and somehow I just had not seen it. My rooms are pitch black at night so maybe I hadn't noticed.

"Is this yours?" J.J. inquired.

Jeff just laughed. J.J. got his answer.

"Nathaniel, come here," J.J. called out again.

"Like he even knows what that is!" Jeff exclaimed, presuming that the same question was meant for him as well. He laughed even harder; but J.J. sat expressionless.

"Is this yours," J.J. inquired.

"No," resounded Nathaniel quickly, "what's it used for?"

"Well, when men and women ..." J.J. began slowly.

"Sexual intercourse. That is the male contraceptive, condom, rubber, raincoat," Jeff said in a medically informed voice and then burst into laughter.

Following suit, Nathaniel soon joined him in laughter on my carpet as J.J. sat stoic, waiting for them to calm down.

"Jeff, Nathaniel," J.J. began, "one time when we lived in D.C. a lady called the house. Dad told me to tell her he wasn't here, and not to tell Mom that she had called at all. One time, it wasn't one condom but a whole roll. He always said he was going to come to the things I was involved in at school—forensics, quiz bowl, whatever else but nope, he never showed up. It all started when I was thirteen. Everything just changed."

Those are all he mentioned and I remembered so much more. He spared many details of many moments that I wish I could forget but rooms can't really choose what goes on within them.

Nathaniel sat, his face twisted in confusion. Then, beginning to cry, he got a tissue from my table and sat back down in the same place, staring into the same space within his mind trying to grasp the new reality before him. Jeff sat as well, but in a different mood. You could see the anger on his face. J.J., knew his temper and tried to console him, but the sound looked to bounce off of him.

As this unfolded, hours earlier I remembered James Sr. putting on a freshly pressed shirt and shortly after Momma left for her all-night shift at the nursing home after working all day as a public school teacher, he took two pieces of plastic protection, slipped them into his pocket and slid out of the backdoor. Before he left, always as before he gave a, "See ya'll after while."

This night was a particularly long *after while* because he didn't come home that night and I'm glad. As J.J. and Nathaniel slept that night, Jeff sat awake sometimes pacing, but sleep did not happen. I stayed up with him, watched him reach into his pocket and find Psalm 37:8, a verse his Momma had given him. She knew what happened when things went wrong and God and Momma were the only things Jeff listened to. "Cease from anger, and forsake wrath: fret not thyself in any wise to do evil" and oh how it looked like he was trying. At seven o'clock in the morning, Momma came home and met J.J. in the door.

He explained what happened as best he could through downward glances and apologetic expressions. Troubled, she asked "Where are they?" He replied, "Nathaniel is still sleep and Jeff is over there pointing to the sofa in the living room that was just big enough for him to stretch all the way out.

Glancing through me towards the sofa, she walked up to Jeff.

"Calm down," she said in a stern but comforting voice.

This had the opposite effect on him as his chest swelled from heavy breathing but no words exited his mouth. He shook his head in disbelief.

"I wanna kill him," he said.

"Jeff," and then gave him a look that spoke volumes in its silence.

"How, Ma? How?"

"I don't know, but I do know that I can't do the same thing. You can't fall because somebody else does," she said staring out into the air, hearing those conversations as concerned relatives told her they saw James Sr. at the local Golden Corral or his truck parked on down a dead end road rocking from the activity within. Later Jeff would understand this conversation but now he just tried to listen.

"Your dad would suck the life out of a flea, but I can't let him suck the life out of me. Proverbs says, *vengeance is mine*. Not yours, but God's. It'll all come out in the wash. Now go get ready for church."

With that she walked into the kitchen and began to make breakfast. Her hands worked quickly to peel potatoes and fry them—crack eggs for omelets and remove bread from the freezer so it could thaw a little before she toasted it. J.J. would only eat potatoes, Nathaniel's eggs only had bacon no cheese, and Jeff would eat both of those and then some. Maybe she would get some rest before church, just ten minutes, but probably not. I watched her do this, her eyes so strong—but was her mind struggling, was she praying silently, asking God to bless her and her family? I'm sure she was. This was routine for her, but I could feel the extra force as she chopped the potatoes—the blade echoing as it struck the tabletop. As she cracked the eggs, yolk spilled as the shell came down too hard over the corner of the bowl. The Lord's Prayer began to escape her lips as she dashed the shakers extra hard into the heated pans between "forgive my trespasses" and "lead me not into temptation." Finally complete, she scraped the rations into their several dishes and left to ready herself.

Everyone ate separately, in between getting ready to go, taking their portion and returning to put on that tie or grab that jacket. After all had eaten, Momma dipped her finger in the bacon grease and rubbed it between her hands and some on her feet. She stared out of my back window that looked out into the backyard. Maybe she's looking at the clothesline that needs to be re-hung, the dilapidated chicken pen that she would like to see harbor chickens again or maybe nothing near that. I'll never know.

"I'm going to the car," her voice echoes through my walls.

Two of the boys hurry to get to the van, but not before gleaning the pans of any stray potatoes and bacon. Far removed the eldest son, J.J., always seemed to oversleep on Sundays now.

Soon after their departure, two trucks rumbled past each other, one up and one down the dirt road. J.J. back to North Carolina, and James Sr. back to me; two generations glaring through windshield glass giving half-hearted waves. The blue and white Ford F-150 took its usual parking spot behind me. A man emerged, that pressed shirt now wrinkled and untucked. Stepping up my six brick steps onto my porch, opening my door and entering, I wished I could turn my locks and bar entry.

He skimmed the empty pans, searching for a second breakfast as it seemed he had already eaten once from the syrup stains on his shirt. Looking content, he turned on the Redskins game and made a home on my sofa. He smelled.

Hearing the rumble of the van that carried his *family* he scurried down my steps into my basement to take a shower and cleanse himself of the events of last evening.

In silence, they all climbed my six brick steps, opened my screen door and went quickly to my bedrooms. No one entered the family room where John Madden and Pat Summerall loudly exclaimed the half-time score.

It was so quiet.

"Don't y'all wanna go play basketball up the road," Momma said slicing the silence. Momma never made pointed suggestions like that, so Jeff and Nathaniel picked up their belongings and left. She discovered J.J. had gone before they returned home from church and before his father had returned as well, as was his way. Momma found his note on her bed looked reflective for a moment and then went on.

"James!" she yelled.

"What?" he yelled back over a microphoned linebacker.

"Come here" she separated the words to stress their importance.

Moments pass and he did not move. Her feet stalked down the hallway and much to James Sr.'s surprise, the television was soon off and instead of beholding offensive lineman, he faced his wife.

"Yes, Anne," as granddaddy used to call her.

"Don't you bring that shit in my house, you understand," a straight forefinger accenting every word.

"But—" he said, trying to enter a word.

"No buts, you keep that filth out of my house."

"But—" again escaped, but it was abbreviated again.

"Did you not hear what I said? Don't do it! I will not have my children seeing that," she interrupted, distraught but so composed continuing. "You just nasty."

"Have you lost your mind?" James Sr. spat in a dumbfounded voice, coming to his feet.

"Have you lost yours?" Momma replied, stepping towards him.

James Sr. had never hit Momma. He was not crazy. In a stammering shuffle he walked out of my back door, slamming it behind him. Momma composed herself and prepared dinner for the kids' return.

Fried chicken was Sunday tradition and Momma was no amateur. Whole breasts were split with bare hands, thighs seared from drumsticks, shaken in batter and thrown into grease. Ritual and routine were at once halted and Momma sat down. Her floured hand rested on her chin and then slid up to her forehead, which began to shake subtly back and forth. I was strong, I thought with my reinforced rafters, concrete foundation and quality brick, but this woman was made out of something different that held her together. I watched it mend her as her eyes flowed back to the present and she continued and completed her tasks. Momma.

With J.J. away with his own family out of tact in North Carolina, Jeff and Nathaniel were left to bear the weight of their father's infidelity. Nathaniel pretended as if nothing was wrong–his way of dealing. He did not act as if anything had changed; conversations were as sparse as they had always been.

That event was the beginning of some trying times for me. Tension escalated with each day - I hated to watch it, as the rift grew larger and larger between a father and his children, a husband and his wife. I could feel the stress pressing against my walls every time Jeff and his father were in the same room—even the dog's ears perked up hoping there wasn't an explosion.

"Good morning, Jeff," James Sr. purged, suggesting that his son should have been the first to speak and recognize his presence.

No words fill the empty air. Jeff just passed by.

I creaked when Jeff and his father brushed passed each other in the hallway, trying to make more room so they wouldn't dare touch. They turned opposite ends of my longest hallway and I knew this was dangerous. Step by step, closer and closer they came, and then their shoulders struck bouncing James Sr. off of my side. Nathaniel, that innocent one, cracks a hidden smile watching from around my corner.

One night, it was particularly heated but only one-sided.

"Who do you think you are?" James, Sr. belted.

Jeff replied with silence, though I did feel his weight bear down into the boards of my belly. He tried to place all of his focus on that page. Lying on the floor in front of my fireplace, he dug a pit amid rising stacks of paper and problems all around him.

"You need me, you know that?" James Sr. ejaculated.

Still, no words from Jeff though his *father* continued.

"You have a nice life, you hear! Let me know how you turn out!" he exploded one last time, and stomped hard on me down my veins towards Momma's bedroom.

"What's that boy's problem?"

"Why don't you ask him?" she responded not looking up from her dinner.

"You know you could change all of this? You could tell them I didn't do anything and it would change."

"Why would I lie to them," she said, glaring at him this time. "I don't lie to my children."

In a stuttering murmur he hustled past Jeff, slammed

my door to the back porch, started his truck and tore away, leaving behind a fog of dust and loose gravel.

Jeff stood and watched the truck tear up the road through the parted curtains in my living room and Momma comes up behind him.

"Are you okay?" she asked.

He nodded his head, smiled and handed her a notepad and he walked away, lay back on my floor and began to write again, even harder than the last time. Just then, she called out to him.

"I want you to read it to me," she said, "come here."

He paused for a moment, but I've never heard him turn down a request to hear him read, and surely he wouldn't say no to Momma.

Jeff asked, "Do you know what it's like to pour your heart into a race, cross the finish line in first place, and look into the crowd and not see your father's face?

Do you know what it's like to be a high school quarterback and make the game-winning throw and look into stands and see only strangers in every row?

Do you know what it's like to be congratulated by a coach after a spectacular game and when he asks, 'where's your father?' and your only reply is 'I don't know?'

Do you know what it's like to play catch by yourself

and see that second glove sitting idle on the shelf? Do you know what it's like to teach yourself to ride a bike and see headlights creep up the wall as Dad returns late at night?

Do you know what it's like to know that the words from your father's mouth are lies and statement by mom have to be verified? Do you know what it's like to dress for church on Sunday morning and no one is there to fix your tie?

Do you know what it's like to accept Christ and as you take your first communion, behind the crowd, see your father walking out?

Do you know what it's like to be neglected, your life rejected, to wish to excel but have no role model to push you in that direction?

Do you know what it's like to see the mother you love so much go down the road of life alone, to persevere through it all and handle a home without one word of encouragement, but instead the spoken hope that she would fail from her spouse?

Do you know what it's like to see mother live in permanent separation while in the same house?

Do you know what it's like to possess so much anger for someone you're supposed to love? Do you know what it's like to pray for strength from above to put that gun down and take off those gloves?

Do you know what it's like to have a father who knows nothing, not one aspect of your life, but boast of your attributes when he has done nothing to help you?

I can only pray to my Heavenly Father as I look to Him tonight that when I have my own sons, they will never ask me, 'Daddy, do you know what it's like?'"

If I could cry I would have, if I could bend my boards and embrace him I would have, but I could do nothing but watch a boy become a man before it was his time.

Within my walls I have seen the tragedies and triumphs of the Jones Family or the Jackson Family depending on which child you're speaking with and if they still claim their father. I have seen, heard, and felt it all; saw James Jr., always the eldest, take his first computer apart and put it back together; saw Jeff compose his first verses on my floor in front of the television; Nathaniel, I marveled as he dove into the Bible, lying somewhere else within me, inhaling its words with blessed understanding, and loved how Momma reared them all. But those are things everybody knew about. Nobody felt J.J.'s knees hit my floor the night granddaddy died or Nathaniel punch a hole in me after being punished after missing basketball practice or the day that changed it all, Friday, March 5, 2000, when the tears of three brothers soaked into my carpet.